Magic Capes, Amazing Powers
Transforming Superhero Play in the Classroom

Eric Hoffman

Redleaf Press
St. Paul, Minnesota
www.redleafpress.org

Published by Redleaf Press
a division of Resources for Child Caring
10 Yorkton Court
St. Paul, MN 55117
Visit us online at www.redleafpress.org

This book is typeset in Minion and designed by Corey Sevett.
Interior illustrations by Nancy Hope
Cover photograph by Ryan Huber Scheife
Cover illustration by Mary Beth Berg

Redleaf Press books are available at a special discount when purchased in bulk (1,000 or more copies) for special premiums and sales promotions. For details, contact the sales manager at 800-423-8309.

Library of Congress Cataloging-in-Publication Data

Hoffman, Eric.
    Magic capes, amazing powers : transforming superhero play in the
classroom / Eric Hoffman.
        p. cm.
Includes index.
    ISBN 1-929610-47-5
1. Education, Preschool—Activity programs. 2. Heroes—Study and
teaching (Preschool)—Activity programs. 3. Violence in
children—Prevention. 4. Multicultural education. 5. Play—Social
aspects. I. Title.
    LB1140.35.C74H52 2004
    372.21—dc22
                                2003025399

11 10 09 08 07 06 05 04   1 2 3 4 5 6 7 8

Magic Capes, Amazing Powers

More Resources from Eric Hoffman

Anti-Bias Books for Kids Series
No Fair to Tigers/No es justo para los tigres
Play Lady/La señora juguetona
Heroines and Heroes/Heroínas y héroes
Best Best Colors/Los mejores colores

Changing Channels: Activities Promoting Media Smarts
and Creative Problem Solving for Children

CONTENTS

Acknowledgments

The activities and quotes found throughout this book come from my own classroom, and from coworkers, parents, and adult students at the Cabrillo College Children's Center and Early Childhood Education Department. My wife, Lisa Kolbeck, who is an expert at facilitating children's language, along with the staff at her Little School Family Day Care Center, also provided examples. Many thanks for your support.

Most of the quotes were either recorded or dictated by children to adults. Some have been edited to shorten them. Others were re-created after the conversation, since teachers don't always have time to write down children's words in the middle of the classroom. These are as true to the original as we could make them.

Since I don't know all the people I have quoted, I have chosen to change everyone's names. I have replaced many of them with the names of my friends and coworkers, to keep myself amused.

Introduction: Summer 1957

I'm seven years old, and I'm dressed for play: red cowboy hat, red bandana, real leather boots, fake leather holsters, and two new silver six-shooter cap guns. It's summer 1957, in the suburbs of Pittsburgh, Pennsylvania. I head outside without saying good-bye and cross the street to Frankie's yard.

Everybody's there: Sam, Rick, Larry, the two Lindas, Annie, and more. Frankie's little brother, Ron, wants to play, too, and his mom says we have to let him. Some days we play kick-the-can or freeze tag, but today it's cowboys and Indians. We choose up good guys and bad guys and decide who gets saved. Ron wants to be a cowboy, but Frankie tells him babies can't be cowboys. The Indians don't want him either, so they pretend to tie him to a stake.

Usually, it's a girl that gets rescued. They take turns, all except for Annie. She's a tomboy. I like Annie, even though she held me down once and spit in my face and laughed.

The cowboys gather behind the hedge. The Indians run to the rock wall and rub dirt on their faces. Ron sits in the middle of the lawn. I practice twirling my guns while we plan the attack. Larry gets tired of talking, so he takes the first shot. Bullets and arrows fly everywhere, and people die, two or three times each. Sam doesn't like dying, but we tell him he has to. Everybody has to take a turn, even scaredy-cats.

I love dying. I can go limp at full speed, bounce off the ground, flip a couple of times, and end up in a heap. I like to make the grown-ups gasp. Today, I'm going to try to kick off my boots on the final spin. I wait until most everybody else is down so I'll have an audience. I make my break into the open lawn. Rick sends an arrow through my chest, and I go out with glory. Maybe I'll be an Indian tomorrow and die falling off a horse, right over the rock wall. Everybody will cheer for that!

All the Indians are dead. Larry is the only cowboy left standing, so he unties Ron. All the cowboys miraculously revive and let out a victory cheer. The Indians lie still, defeated again.

We play five rounds before dinner. The Indians win one, which happens sometimes when Larry is chief. Then the Indians get to whoop and dance, and somebody has to burn. Today, it's Ron.

———————————————

Forty-plus years later, I'm wondering what I learned in Frankie's yard. Cooperation, negotiation, imagination, how I could be a leader and a follower, how far I could push my body, and how I compared to my peers. I got to think about death without getting too scared, the way I sometimes did at night, and I got to try out being powerful in a very big and confusing world. These are valuable lessons for a growing child.

But I learned some other lessons as well, ones that I've had to work hard to unlearn: that Native Americans are bloodthirsty monsters who scalp people and dance around like monkeys; that bad guys have dark faces; that big boys are always the leaders, and girls and little kids the victims; that TV is the best place to get ideas for play; and that guns and violence solve problems. This same misinformation is still part of the world our children enter. In fact, some of these messages have gotten stronger in the last forty years. Are these the lessons I want to pass on to the children in my care?

When I first started working with young children in the early seventies, my mentors emphasized a golden rule: trust children's play. Play is the concrete expression of children's wonder. It allows children to explore ideas and share them with friends. It wraps each child's questions and answers into one natural learning process, a process that works best when undisturbed. A good teacher observes, facilitates, and intervenes to keep everything safe, but always honors the play.

With the rise of the anti-bias approach to teaching, the teacher's role has become more complex. While play is still considered central in early childhood education, the cultural context of that play cannot be ignored. Our responsibility for keeping children safe has expanded beyond taking care of children's immediate physical and emotional needs. We must now be aware of the ways a child's long-term identity can be damaged by racism, sexism, and other forms of bias, and how play can reinforce these misconceptions and lies. Our job is to find effective ways to intervene and challenge the bias without destroying the play. How do we balance children's developmental need for uninterrupted play with our desire to work against prejudice and violence?

Superhero play is one of the places where this dilemma becomes real. While many children love it, many adults worry about the lessons children might be learning from it, such as these:

* Differences are threatening
* Conflicts must always be "won"
* Dominance and aggression are appropriate ways to win and maintain power
* Weapons are the magic keys to power and victory
* Toys are the magic keys to happiness

I want to keep children from being exposed to this vision of the world, as would most of the parents and teachers I talk to. A huge part of the solution would be to keep the images and stories that reinforce these beliefs away from children's eyes, ears, and minds. We don't have that power.

So what are adults supposed to do? Some give up and ignore the play, hoping for the best. Some ban it. But there is another alternative, one that guides the play and uses it to introduce positive values while respecting the needs and concerns of all involved.

This approach can show children how to use power wisely, understand the difference between real violence and pretend violence, settle conflicts without hurting anyone, and act with compassion when others need help. It's not always easy to achieve, and it takes more time than restricting the play. It can only happen if you take children's points of view seriously, and incorporate their issues into your daily curriculum.

Sometimes it's difficult to hold on to a positive vision of the future when we're worried about our children, but we have to keep it in mind. Young children use our vision as a guide when they create their own dreams for the future. They are building a picture of how the world works, of how people relate to each other and to our planet. They are learning what people do to feel powerful and how people who have power use it. They are exploring how to handle their fears and desires. While we can shield them for a short time from those who abuse their authority, sooner or later they will confront violence, racism, and other corruptions of power, both in the media and in the real world. Superhero play is a way children say to us, "I want to know more about these things. I want to know what I should do about them. What can you teach me?" When we ignore their play, we are telling them that we have no worthwhile answers to their questions, and that the answers they get from the TV and the toy store are the best ones around. When we ban the play, we are telling them that their questions scare us, and that the best thing to do when you're afraid of a question is to stop the person from asking it. Neither of these choices provides a good model for young children to carry as they become teenagers and young adults.

This book documents what I and other teachers have learned as we have looked for a path that respects children's needs while providing a way for adults to express their concerns and keep children safe. First, we'll look at what superhero play is and what draws children to it. Next we'll look at the many reasons adults find this play troublesome. The rest of the book documents classroom strategies and curriculum that can help you transform superhero play into a welcome part of your curriculum. I hope these ideas will give you the seeds to develop your own positive approach to superhero play.

CHAPTER 1

Understanding Superhero Play

"I like to be Superman because he's a big guy, and big guys have the power. They can do lots of things, and they never die."

—Eddie, age three

WHY ARE CHILDREN like Eddie so fascinated with superhero play? Why do some children insist on sleeping in their superhero costumes, with pretend weapons by their sides? Why are they willing to defy restrictions on their play by biting crackers into gun shapes when we're not looking? For answers, we'll look at several questions that will help us understand superhero play:

- ★ How is superhero play different from other forms of dramatic play? How is it the same?
- ★ How does gender influence superhero play?
- ★ Why do children get involved in superhero play?

What Is Superhero Play?

Anyone who has spent time with preschoolers has witnessed scenes like the ones in the following list. Which would you call superhero play?

- ★ Monsters baring their claws and teeth as they lurch across the lawn
- ★ Two Batmans, a Pokemon, one Superwoman, and various robots—all wearing capes and shooting rolled-up paper guns
- ★ Space aliens digging on the moon for treasure
- ★ Two forest fairies and a witch preparing magic spells and poison potions to make their friends disappear
- ★ Army action figures on a search-and-destroy mission
- ★ Knights in armor swinging swords at fire-breathing dragons
- ★ Martial arts experts twirling and kicking on top of the climbing structure
- ★ Princes and princesses issuing orders to everyone around them
- ★ "Good guys" and "bad guys" fighting each other with every kind of high-tech and low-tech weapon imaginable

For the purposes of this book, all of these are considered superhero play. They all involve play that centers on children's fantasies of danger, bravery, good and evil, and above all, power. In superhero play, children don't just mimic adult activities, they become larger-than-life characters that help them explore their fears, hopes, and passions. They use imaginative stories and props that symbolize these feelings.

Superhero play is one type of dramatic play (some teachers refer to dramatic play as make-believe play). Other kinds include family and home play (for example, cooking or baby care), occupational play (for example, post office or grocery store), and nature play (for example, butterflies or kittens). Most children participate in some form of dramatic play in their preschool years, but not all preschoolers get involved in superhero play. While signs of dramatic play can be seen even among one-year-olds, sustained play based on fantasy characters and stories usually appears when children are in preschool. It's a sign that their brains have developed enough to think about the past and the future, and to picture what it's like to be someone or somewhere else. These abilities are beyond the grasp of infants. As their mental abilities grow, dramatic play becomes a way children can let their imaginations flourish and share exciting new ideas with friends.

How Is Superhero Play Different from Other Forms of Dramatic Play?

In all varieties of dramatic play, children take on new identities, becoming a crying baby, a busy parent, a pony galloping with its herd, or an airplane pilot. These roles may be inspired by children's observations, stories in books, TV shows, or movies, or they may be completely made-up. Characters can even be based on inanimate objects, since what is alive and not alive is one of the questions children are exploring at this age.

> *Look at me, I'm a blender*
> —Megan, age four, while twirling and spinning a scarf above her head

The roles children take during dramatic play may be realistic, such as babies, truck drivers, and teachers, or they may be imaginary. Most of the roles in superhero play come from fantasy images, like dragons, monsters, and fairies, or from heroic or mythic characters, like firefighters, kings, and queens. This role playing provides a way for children to "think out loud" and gain a deeper understanding of what they have observed or imagined. They get to practice adult skills, explore feelings, try out new ways to connect with friends, discover how their bodies move, and try to make sense of the large, and sometimes baffling, world around them.

One of the hallmarks of all forms of dramatic play is the use of costumes and props. Materials can range from a few pebbles to elaborately arranged furniture and scenery. Children don't need mountains of toys and costumes for dramatic play to succeed. In fact, make-believe works best when children are required to use their creativity and communication skills to keep the game alive. A few sticks, a blanket, a box, and a time and place to use them are all that some children need to stay engaged in dramatic play for hours. While most dramatic play props allow children to practice real-life skills like feeding a dog, talking on a phone, or fixing a car, superhero props support exploration of other, more complex aspects of growing up: adult power, independence, and control.

Superheroes use capes, power bracelets, wings, masks, magic wands, costumes that exaggerate human or animal features, and the ultimate power symbols—guns and other weapons.

Dramatic play becomes more complex and organized as children get older. Two-year-olds' dramatic play is usually based on imitation, and is done alone or in loosely organized small groups, with few rules:

> *Four toddlers cook with sand together. Two are making birthday cakes and blowing out candles, one is cooking soup, while the other is making tortillas to feed the teacher.*

Four-year-olds like to play in larger groups, with more inventive materials, roles, and rules. Some still do their dramatic play alone, while others create imaginary friends. Discussing what the game looks like can take as much time as playing the game itself, and the play can change quickly:

> *Five preschoolers build a structure out of boxes while arguing about whether it's a ship or a doghouse. Two of them end up as babies under blankets, while their "mother" and two "brothers" cook poison stew inside an old tire. They invite a friend in to be a kitten on a leash, while telling another child who wants to be the father to go away. Fifteen minutes later, the rejected child has joined the group, driving into the woods to look for lost puppies.*

School-age games can stick to the same fantasy theme for hours and take over an entire playground.

> *A team of seven-year-old adventurers go sailing in their boats. They fish for tuna, squid, and sharks; go diving for pearls, sunken treasure, and shark teeth; get attacked by sharks; fight the pirates who are trying to steal their gold . . . and feed them to the sharks.*

Like other dramatic play, superhero play gets more intricate as children get older and their imaginations expand:

> A two-year-old points her shovel at a bird and shouts, "Bang!" Three others join her, all walking in different directions, shooting at trees, chairs, and friends.

> Six four-year-olds play a chase game. Each is a caped superhero from a different TV show or movie. Two of them decide the others are bad guys. They catch one and lead him to jail under the climbing structure. He starts to cry—that's not what he thought was supposed to happen in this game.

> A group of seven- and eight-year-olds play space fighters. Some have made "laser razors" out of cardboard tubes and space helmets out of paper bags. One is the commander, and he orders an attack on the painted cardboard box that has become the alien spaceship. The aliens protest; they thought they were flying to find treasure on Mars. The game stops while the teams argue about it, until the commander convinces the space fighters and aliens to join forces, travel back in time, and blow up a wormhole being used by raiders from another galaxy. Their victory is short-lived; photon rays have set their energy transformers on fire!

At circle time I asked a group of four-year-olds, "What makes someone a superhero?" We made a list, which I posted on a bulletin board. Several children added pictures to illustrate their ideas:

What Makes Someone a Superhero?
- They fight bad guys.
- They kill bad guys.
- They kill monsters.
- They fight trouble.
- They shoot the evil.
- They jump over buildings, even the whole school.
- They can break the whole school if they want to, but they don't.
- They're so strong, they could pick up the whole school and throw it across the ocean, and it would crash, but we would still be inside and we wouldn't get hurt.
- Sometimes they can be girls, right?
- They help people when criminals and robbers get them.
- They don't hurt people.
- They don't hurt animals.
- They save all the people and all the animals.
- Good guys save the planet.
- Good guys save the Earth.
- Good guys save the whole Earth and all the people and all the animals and all the trees and all the animals.
- They can't die, but if they die, they can be alive again.
- They have treasure in their hearts that makes them good.
- They find treasure, they know where it is because God tells them.
- God tells them to be good.
- They don't get afraid.
- When something scary happens, like a monster, they just say, "Huh!"
- They're the good guys.

How Does Gender Influence Superhero Play?

Throughout most of this book, I purposely present information on play that is gender neutral, and use examples and quotations from both boys and girls. But no discussion of this topic can be complete if the issue of gender difference is ignored. Differences in the ways boys and girls play are seen around the world. Preschool superhero play is one place these disparities are clear, with boys and girls often taking different roles and engaging in very different activities. Many teachers and parents believe that girls rarely get involved in superhero play.

Witches, princesses, stepmothers, magic potions, and fairies are common in the fantasy play of young girls. While many people don't think of this as superhero play, I include it in this book because girls use it to explore many of the same issues boys do when they are chasing and shooting monsters. Adults may find feminine images less worrisome than male-identified ones, because the symbols are borrowed from traditional fairy tales and don't mimic real-world violence as much. Nonetheless, scary villains, superpowers, and death are still important to the play of many girls.

> *Allison, age five: The wicked vampire put his power in my breast. It's really scary. The sister died, and I got the poison apple.*
>
> *Lily, age four: The good queen dies.*
>
> *Allison: Yes, the good queen dies. And there's a flying bird after me! He gets into stone 'cause his cape is stone. The princess thinks it's a prince, 'cause he has a sword. She falls asleep but the prince has his arm around her.*
>
> *Lily: 'Member that Hansel and Gretel?*
>
> *Allison: That story doesn't have a poison apple. The prince is under a spell, so she thinks it's her friend but it really isn't.*
>
> *Lily: Some people are under spells—the mean queen and the mommy queen. The good queen wants to dress like a bad queen 'cause she likes it.*

The different styles of boy and girl play don't have hard and fast boundaries. As with many other gender stereotypes, plenty of children undermine them by breaking the mold. Witches, fairies, and magic wands can appear in boy's play.

> *Randy, age four: How about we go on a fairy vacation? How about our wands are waterproof, right?*
>
> *Armand, age four: I don't need any wands because I'm full of fairy dust.*
>
> *Randy: Pretend we're going to the witch's haunted house, right? And we make it disappear.*
>
> *Armand: It's spooky inside! Better get out before it turns into fire.*
>
> *Randy: And we go to sleep.*
>
> *Armand: No! If there's a nighttime here, I'm not playing.*
>
> *Randy: Okay, there's only going to bed in the daytime here.*

And guns and bad guys can show up in girl's play.

> *Gwen, age four: (On the climbing structure) This is the Powerpuff board. It kills the other guys, but not me. I'm a rough guy.*
>
> *Sally, age three: I'm not a rough guy, I'm a bad guy.*
>
> *Gwen: Don't step here! It's rough! You'll die! The bad guy board is over there.*
>
> *Renata, age four: We're all bad guys. Here's our sword (a piece of a plant). Bad guys!*
>
> *Everyone: (Marching) Bad guys! Bad guys! Bad guys! Shoot! Shoot! Shoot!*
>
> *Sally: And we're aliens, right?*
>
> *Gwen: Right! And our guns work!*
>
> *Everyone: Our guns work! Our guns work! Our guns work!*

Here are two group poems that illustrate the differences often seen in superhero play between boys and girls. They were created by a teacher who asked children questions during the play, then wrote down the answers in poem form.

Two boys were arguing about who was the strongest superhero. The teacher asked them, "What can a strong person do?"

I'm So Strong

by Daniel and Arthur, age four

I'm so strong I could kill a witch
   a mom
   a water buffalo.

I'm so strong I could lift a trailer from a truck
   a big big heavy truck.
   I could fight a big pirate ship.

We're the bee guys, the bee guys.
The bee guys are bad guys.

I could lift everything heavy up at one time.
I'm so strong I could cook.
I'm so strong I could lift a tree
   a sword
   a whole house.

Only Daniel and Arthur can be strong.
I'm stronger than you
You're stronger than me
But I'm stronger than my body.

The same teacher asked a group of girls who were arguing about who was the most beautiful to describe their game. Here's what they said:

The Light Princesses

by Maria, Vanna, and Cindy, age four

We're the light princesses
so light
that the wind might blow us up.
The blood presses
a special button in our hearts
so the wind won't
blow us away forever.
We went to the Prince's house to see our brother
our Prince that loves us so much.
We're going to dance now!
Our capes make the wind
blow us beautiful.
We've got wings on our backs.
You don't see us but
you hear us.
We're the angel's friends.

Why Do Children Get Involved in Superhero Play?

To young children, adults' abilities and powers seem magical. Superhero play lets children try out how it feels to be "big." Superheroes are larger than life, just as adults appear to be. They take charge, make decisions, solve problems, and think about some very grown-up ideas, like power, wisdom, bravery, and fairness. Before we can help children create a positive vision of what it means to be grown-up, we have to know more about what they are looking for when they put on a cape or pick up a magic wand. Children get involved in superhero play for reasons that cover all aspects of their growth: physical, mental, spiritual, social, and emotional. Superhero play attracts children who are

★ Investigating power and autonomy
★ Balancing the desire for power with the need for friendship
★ Testing physical limits
★ Exploring feelings

★ Answering "big questions" about the world, such as these:

What is right and what is wrong, good and bad?

What is fair and what is unfair?

What is life and what is death?

What is a boy and what is a girl?

What is real and what is fantasy?

Children work hard to gather this information. They watch people at home, at school, in the community, and on TV, and they imitate what they see. They listen to our words and pay attention to our body language. They ask us for details, test our limits to see if we mean what we say, and make lots of guesses. They imagine what being a grown-up is like, and then play out what they have envisioned. These topics and questions don't have easy answers, even for adults. Preschoolers are just beginning to grapple with them. The information young children discover in this research colors the way they view the world for the rest of their lives.

Investigating Power and Autonomy

Power is important to American preschoolers. Family, teachers, media, and peers tell them that independence is essential. They want to know how to take control, and how to use that control to get what they want. They want to know who is in charge, who makes decisions, and who gets attention. They want to check out what is an acceptable use of power, who gets to make the rules, and how those rules will be enforced. While they still want someone to take care of them and keep them safe, they don't like feeling powerless or humiliated.

Power can be tricky to understand. Every culture and social group has its own intricate and often unspoken rules about it, and these rules are rarely logical. Young children learn them by observing, testing, and imitating. They are not interested in abstract ideas; they are looking for practical information. How do adults act when they have power? How do their behaviors, posture, and speech change when they don't? How do they get what they want when a more powerful person says no? What makes people cooperative or competitive, friendly or fearful, and how do people use these emotions to motivate others? How do objects like guns, uniforms, and money make people more powerful? Do age, appearance, skin color, and gender make a difference? It takes a lot of effort to investigate these issues; by the time they reach kindergarten, every child deserves a college degree in cultural studies.

Here's how one five-year-old classroom leader, Howard, found out where he stood with Jim, a new assistant director who had been on the job for two weeks.

Howard: Who are you? I've seen you here before.

Jim: I'm Jim.

Howard: No, I mean, what's your job?

Jim: I'm the assistant director.

Howard: No, I mean, whose boss are you? Judy [the teacher] is the boss of the kids. She gets to tell Joanne [the aide] what to do too. Nancy [the director] is the big boss. She gets to tell the teachers what to do. So whose boss are you?

Jim: I help Nancy. I help the big boss.

Howard: So do you get to tell me what to do?

Jim: If you're not being safe, I'll help you stop.

Howard: [Expletive]! Everybody around here gets to tell me what to do!

All of their studying comes back to one question: How much power do I have? The answer is confusing. Three- and four-year-olds have conquered some huge developmental mountains. They have learned to walk and talk and use the toilet. They are learning to dress, feed, and clean themselves. They have a pretty clear idea of how the world works within their own home and family. While they still need the comfort and assistance of adults, they don't want to be considered babies anymore. "Baby" becomes an insult at this age, a swear word that can reduce a young child to tears. Many modern preschoolers believe that they are truly grown-up, ready to take on the whole world—until they look around and discover what a big, bewildering world it is.

Many of our young children grow up in communities where they don't know everyone, where public spaces are full of unknown people doing strange things. Even in communities that are small enough for everyone to know everybody's name, TV can bring strangers directly into a child's home. Some children enjoy this experience and some are afraid of it, either because of their temperament or because adults have modeled these reactions. Either way, when children start to pay more attention to the world outside their families, they find there is much they don't understand. So at the same time that they start feeling in command of themselves and their environment, young children discover that they are small and powerless in the larger picture. Is it any wonder that today's preschoolers look for the most powerful images they can find to act out in their play?

As part of superhero play, preschoolers experiment with roles that explore all sides of the power equation. They become heroes, victims, and bad guys. They try out being tricksters, rebels, monsters, champions, bullies, babies, clowns, kings, and queens. They try being powerful alone and as part of a team. All of these roles allow children to practice different ways of taking control of their lives and their feelings.

Preschoolers like to imitate powerful people—real people who make things happen, like parents, firefighters, and doctors, and fantasy characters, like superheroes, fairy godmothers, and dragons. They love stories that show characters like Cinderella or the Three Little Pigs, who start out powerless but use their physical strength, wits, or beauty to overcome danger. They want to hear tales of people and animals who transform into powerful beings. And they love to use the tools of power these stories spotlight— guns, swords, secret potions, magic wands, fantastic vehicles, jewels, capes, and crowns.

Learning about power also means trying out a variety of ways to take charge with friends and family. Toddlers and preschoolers will use any physical, verbal, or mental approach that works to get what they want, especially in the middle of superhero play. Some of their strategies may be hurtful. They have not yet developed an internal set of moral standards to guide them, so they need adults to help them learn strategies that are safe for everyone.

Balancing the Desire for Power with the Need for Friendship

Does this interest in control and autonomy mean that preschoolers won't show any regard for anyone else's feelings or safety? Certainly not. Children also want people to like them, care about them, and play with them. They want relationships with adults who will help them and teach them. They like to help others and feel like they are a good friend. But sometimes this need for relationships conflicts with their desire for power.

> *Bonnie, age three: Can I play with you? Are you my friend?*
>
> *Lenore, age four: Yes, but you have to be the baby. I'm the momma.*
>
> *Bonnie: No, I don't want to be a baby. I want to be a momma too.*
>
> *Lenore: No, there's only one momma. You have to be the baby and you have to do what I say.*
>
> *Bonnie: I don't want to be a baby. I'm not a baby.*
>
> *Lenore: Then you can't play. You're not my friend.*

Bonnie: You never let me! I hate you! (She pushes the dishes off the table and runs away.)

The need for relationships with other people, and the struggle to balance those connections with the desire for power, is another major theme underlying superhero play. One of the primary challenges of this age is for children to use their developing ability to predict, plan, and control events in order to support their friendships rather than destroy them, by learning how to negotiate, cooperate, and compromise. As teachers of young children are aware, play can become a constant power struggle if they don't learn those lessons, with each child using whatever force they possess to keep control. Many well-meaning attempts at friendship end in frustration and disaster. Blending relationship and autonomy is a challenge that doesn't ever go away—even some adults need assistance with it. Superhero play helps children explore this challenge. Why does this issue become so important in the preschool years?

Children are interested in human relationships from the time they are born. They have to be! With no words and very little body control, newborns depend on other humans to take care of their needs and keep them safe. Crying, sucking, rocking, and making faces are all ways to communicate those needs to caregivers. Without a close attachment to at least one adult, growing up becomes difficult—how can you help others learn to take care of you when no one is there to watch, touch, listen, and respond?

As infants grow into toddlers, an internal struggle begins. Toddlers want to go places — to the back of the bushes and the bottom of the hill and the top of the couch. They want to learn new words, and sing them twenty times a minute to anyone who will listen. They want to do things themselves. As they use their newly acquired mobility and language to discover the world, the feelings of independence and competence can be exhilarating.

They can also be frightening. Toddlers want to explore—but with caregivers close by to keep them safe. Staying connected to adults becomes a complex dance. Eye contact, facial expressions, and simple language help them keep in touch with important people when new experiences draw them away. A new rhythm gets established—go off to play, look back to make sure the adult is still there, move further away to test the boundaries, come back for a hug.

"No" becomes an important word in this dance. When a toddler wants autonomy, it is an excellent tool for setting up boundaries between me and you. Some two-year-olds can be very assertive when they want to let adults know they need some separation.

Ismael, age two, screams, "No!" and pretends to shoot his mother's face with his bottle when she tries to take it from him, even though there is nothing left in it. She gets angry, and he cries. After the struggle, he wants to be in her arms.

For some children, the beginning of superhero and weapons play lies in their desire to be separate from their caregivers and make their own decisions. Some children are attracted to weapons play for this very reason—they know it creates distance between themselves and the adults, because the adults don't like it.

By preschool, children can keep in touch with their caregivers in a whole new way—by holding an image of them in their minds. Their brains have developed to the point where they can visualize people in other times and places. Three-year-olds often ask a lot of questions to clarify these mental images. Where are you when I'm asleep or when I'm playing in another room? What are you doing when I'm at school? Where are you going to be later today, or tomorrow? Children can get very anxious during this learning process, and they can cling and whine, but in the end they are able to spend longer periods away from important adults without physical contact.

Using mental images to keep their relationships with adults going allows preschoolers to pay attention to a different set of relationships—the ones with their peers. Friendships become a major focus at this age, as well as a source of great joy and distress. If someone plays with you, it is a sign of a successful friendship. If not, the friendship is over. Four-year-olds delight in coming up with new ways to play together, and they can be deeply hurt when the play falls apart.

Sustaining friendships can be difficult for preschoolers. Toddlers usually engage in parallel play, staying near each other without having to agree on any game. Preschoolers and kindergartners are ready for more complex friendships, but that brings up a whole new set of problems to solve. Who gets to decide what happens during the play? How does everyone know what to do? What is the "story" that guides the game? How do you get everyone to change that vision in the middle of the game if you have a new idea?

When young children start playing together in groups, their first attempts at answering these questions are often self-centered and crude. Compromise means incorporating another person's opinions into your own, but preschoolers have a hard time explaining their thoughts to their friends or understanding that their friends can have other ideas. They can get very angry when others don't play the game "the right way." For many preschoolers, compromise is threatening because it means giving up their newfound autonomy—if I accept someone else's ideas, my own ideas might disappear.

One way children solve this problem is by creating games with a few simple rules that everyone can understand. The simplest is Chase. It's easy to learn, easy to organize, uses lots of energy, and children can come and go as they please. While older children play Chase as a competitive game, younger children tend to use it to build a sense of connection among the players. Pretending to shoot at each other while chasing is another way children can stay connected, clarify who is in the game, and maintain the excitement. It becomes a shorthand way to say, "I'm still playing. Are you?" Once everybody in a group understands the basic rules of Chase, children start to add new props, like costumes and weapons, and new roles, like good guys, bad guys, and victims.

While the rules of Chase may seem obvious, situations arise that still create conflict. For example, a child will throw a ball at others who are chasing her and an argument will erupt, because no one has talked about what happens then. Do you die if you get hit by the ball? Throw it back? Who decides?

As Chase gets more complex, it requires more and more communication to make sure everyone understands the game. Shared, repetitive superhero stories make relationships easier to maintain by allowing children to try more elaborate games without a lot of negotiation.

Television shows and movies (along with the mythologies and folktales found in many cultures) make this process even easier, since everyone who watches the same show starts out with some knowledge of the game. They provide a communal vision that allows everyone to make social connections without the need for endless talk. Any child could walk onto a playground in the eighties, call out "Ninja Turtles!" and have a fun game going in a minute. In the nineties, Power Rangers ruled. Children who have never seen these shows learn very quickly how to fake it so they can be included. Some of my most fanatic Digimon and Pokemon players were never allowed to watch the show! The desire to have successful connections with peers is so strong that it can drive children to learn the art of lying.

Anxiety about maintaining both relationships and independence is an underlying theme in children's play at any age. When superhero play is done safely, it can be a valuable way for beginners to balance these competing drives, because it combines them into a single game that is exciting, easy to play, and helps the children bond as a group. The fact that it bothers some adults is an added bonus!

Testing Physical Limits

Many children get involved in superhero play because they want to test and expand the limits of their physical abilities. That's what their growing bodies are telling them to do! By their fourth birthday, most children have mastered control of their large muscle groups. Walking, which used to be such a challenge, is now a bore—why not run or jump?

Teacher, to a group of superheroes: No running in the classroom, please!

Luz, age three: But teacher, we're not good at walking.

Some preschoolers go through a phase when they drive adults crazy by running everywhere. When they start, they run like wobbly toddlers—knees and elbows going in all directions. Six weeks later, they've got the straight-ahead, no-wasted-motion run of a kindergartner. All it took was practice.

Along with speed, children want to improve their strength, accuracy, coordination, and balance. Superheroes, especially the ones on TV and in the movies, are attractive models, because they use all of these talents. Twirling, kicking, rolling, jumping, throwing, punching—watching superheroes is like watching the Olympics every day. While adults understand that many of the gymnastics portrayed in the media are done with special effects, safety equipment, and animation, children assume that what they see is real. They can see it with their own eyes, can't they? So they do what they always do when they want to learn a new and interesting skill: they methodically observe, imitate, and practice. Adults have been shocked to find that young children can, in fact, do some of the seemingly impossible tricks they see on the screen, moving in ways that would send an adult to the emergency room.

Roughhousing is another common component of superhero play. Wrestling, tackling, bouncing off each other with abandon, and rolling around like puppies—it's a great way for children to get the body contact and stimulation they crave, especially those boys who have been given the message that males shouldn't be affectionate with each other. Superhero play provides a convenient framework for children who want to roughhouse.

Exploring Feelings

Here is a list of words taken from children's fantasy play:

- ★ Monster
- ★ Pirates
- ★ Death trap
- ★ Sharks
- ★ Fire
- ★ Tornado
- ★ Bomb
- ★ Hot lava rifle
- ★ Goblin
- ★ Robber killers

- ★ Bloody poison
- ★ War
- ★ Dangerous emergency

All of these words have anger and fear behind them. Here are some other images from children's fantasy play:

- ★ Golden treasures
- ★ King and queen
- ★ Prince and princess
- ★ Hero and heroine
- ★ Superfriend
- ★ Magic seeds
- ★ Captain of the planet
- ★ Spirit of mystery
- ★ Rescue patrol
- ★ Crystal hearts
- ★ Magic rainbow
- ★ Unicorn

These words are filled with hope, passion, wonder, and bravery. Young children want to know more about all of these feelings. Superhero play helps children turn feelings into symbols that can be explored through play. Interest in using play materials this way blossoms in the preschool years. Why?

Children's minds and imaginations are expanding as they enter preschool, but this growth has both rewards and challenges. Infants and toddlers don't have many fears of the unknown, because they can't picture the unknown. Preschoolers and kindergartners can. The capacity to visualize the past and future plunges young children into emotions that they have never had to navigate. They can imagine having new friends, but they also know that their friends might reject them tomorrow. They can picture saving someone from harm, and they can imagine getting hurt and possibly dying in an accident. They can fill the spaces under beds and inside closets with fairy godmothers and monsters. Fantasies can be fun—but they can be scary when they're out of control. Fear and anxiety become particularly potent emotions at this age.

> *Gloria, age three: It's a vampire monster! See it?*
>
> *Cathy, age three: You scared?*
>
> *Gloria: It's scary! But not really, right? It's pretending, right?*

Cathy: It is?

Gloria: It is?

Preschoolers don't talk about these feelings in abstract terms, though. Instead, they turn them into concrete images that can be manipulated through play. Even though they have become much more skilled with language, most young children prefer to express themselves through action. Keep in mind that the first language children learn is not spoken language, but body language. As infants, they read feelings and intentions by paying attention to our actions, touch, facial expressions, and voice intonations. Even when children are old enough to understand the value of words, they still don't depend on them, because bodies tell more than words. That's why so many young children feel compelled to test our spoken rules by breaking them and watching our reactions. So when preschoolers want to understand feelings, they turn them into roles, props, and actions that can be investigated through fantasy play.

Children choose superhero play more than any other type of dramatic play when they want to focus on feelings. When children pretend to cook or drive a car, they are imitating adult actions. When they battle bad guys, they are not necessarily practicing future acts of violence (although this can be an element for some children—see the chapter on adult concerns for further discussion). Fantasy monsters are most often symbols that represent children's fear, worry, and anger. Magic wands, weapons, and superpowers are the symbolic tools they use to take control of those emotions and feel safe, powerful, and alive. Children use superhero play to figure out how to overcome fear, handle anger, create joy and pride, and live with passion. They explore when to be assertive and when it is more appropriate to be passive. They create a road map of their emotions, and discover acceptable ways to communicate them. All of that is necessary before children can learn to empathize with the feelings and points of view of others, an ability that is crucial for children to develop if they want satisfying friendships.

Answering "Big Questions" about the World

Along with a desire to explore their feelings, preschoolers are ready to tackle some major intellectual and spiritual questions. As Jeanine (age four) put it, "Sometimes I have little questions and sometimes I have a big fat question." Their newly developed mental abilities allow them to think about these important issues:

★ What is right and wrong, good and bad?
★ What is fair and what is unfair?
★ What is life and what is death?
★ What is a boy and what is a girl?
★ What is real and what is fantasy?

More than any other play, superhero play touches on all these big questions. Play is not only the way children express feelings, it is also the method children use to test their theories about how the world works.

Unlike adults, who tend to ignore information that contradicts their beliefs, young children seek new experiences that will clarify their ideas. Then they reinvestigate their questions from the beginning and come up with a new set of beliefs. They don't do this research by sitting quietly in thought; their methods are action-oriented, designed to test out their ideas in the world of play.

Big Questions: What Is Right and Wrong, Good and Bad?

Young children want to figure out the difference between right and wrong. To adults, the distinction may seem obvious, but it can be baffling to preschoolers. They may be able to repeat adult definitions of these labels, but they don't necessarily understand them. They know that caregivers have told them that some of their behaviors are good and should be repeated, while some are bad and should be stopped, but they are not yet able to make consistent choices based on a set of internal moral beliefs. They are starting to question whether adult words and actions are always true and good. The information they get from the media adds to their confusion.

Betty Lou, age five: I'm a good guy! I'm a good guy!

Teacher: What do good guys do?

Betty Lou: They shoot bad guys.

Teacher: What do bad guys do?

Betty Lou: They shoot good guys.

Teacher: So everybody shoots each other. How can you tell which ones are good and which ones are bad?

Betty Lou: The good guys win.

Teacher: Is that the way it works on TV?

Betty Lou: Yes.

Parents start labeling children's behavior as good and bad during the late toddler years. When people talk about a "good" baby, they usually mean one that is easy to care for. Most adults (although, sadly, not all) don't label infant behavior as a moral choice that the baby makes. And while parents may try to change a newborn's behavior, they don't usually expect their baby to sort out right from wrong.

We have different expectations of preschoolers. Preschoolers are able to understand and speak about concepts far beyond what they could comprehend just a few years earlier. But this huge jump in language and thought development can fool us into believing preschoolers understand more about abstract moral concepts than they do. Their thinking has expanded, but it is still very connected to the practical and concrete. Actions are "good" if they work to get you what you want, and "bad" if they make your parents or friends angry. People are "good" if they win, and "bad" if they look scary or strange. Breaking rules becomes one way to see whether adults really mean what they say about right and wrong.

They are most interested in answering a practical question—am I a good person or a bad person? Does having a different opinion from my parents make me bad? What if I throw a tantrum, or hurt someone? Does breaking a toy by accident carry the same moral weight as breaking it on purpose? How about pretending to break it? What if I mix up a pretend poison potion for a classmate I don't like? If I'm bad, what do I have to do to be considered good again? Can I be both good and bad? And what about things like bad manners? By the time children enter the elementary grades, these kinds of questions have helped form their values and self-concepts.

Many adults would like to believe there is only one correct set of answers to questions of right and wrong, and that those answers should be clear to even the youngest child. While there is certainly agreement among most people about basic moral boundaries, different families and societies define good and bad in very different ways. Whether we agree with these beliefs or not, we can't expect children to understand right and wrong without their usual learning process—observation, imitation, testing adult expectations, and play.

Superheroes are a perfect match for children who want to discover more about right and wrong through play. Trying out good guy, bad guy, and victim roles; testing limits; pretending to do noble and evil deeds; helping others; and allowing others to come to your rescue fosters moral development by giving preschoolers experiences on which to build abstract concepts. Letting children actually hurt other people is a very different story; adults need to give clear messages about what is safe and acceptable, both physically and emotionally. This is especially important when children receive confusing and contradictory moral messages from media and advertising.

Big Questions: What Is Fair and What Is Unfair?

As children learn more about power and about right and wrong, they become interested in the related issue of justice, what is fair and what is not. Like their ideas of right and wrong, a preschooler's sense of justice is often quite self-centered: I can change the rules of a game if it helps me win; I can divide a cookie unevenly if it means I get the portion I want; if I don't like what you are doing to me, then that's not fair, even if it is exactly what I just did to you.

Nancy, age three: I want the yellow one [a truck].

Julie, age three: I'm using it.

Nancy: (Grabs the truck) You have to share.

Julie: No! (Grabs it back.)

Nancy: No fair!

In this example, Nancy feels fine about grabbing the truck, but it's unacceptable when Julie grabs it back.

These early ideas of fairness can seem selfish and whiny, so many adults respond by ignoring them, or even punishing children. But when we silence children who are just starting to think about fairness, we are missing an opportunity to help them develop a more mature concept of justice, one that respects the perspectives and needs of others. Children learn that only power matters, so when powerful adults aren't around to police the action, size and strength are what count. And when adults are present, the best way to get what you want is to manipulate them into taking your side. Some children become experts at that!

Preschoolers are just beginning to gain awareness of the problems that exist in the larger world. Their ideas about justice aren't based on the big issues of the day, but on the ways adults treat them during small, daily conflicts. By encouraging all the children in a conflict to express their ideas about fair solutions, and helping them agree to solutions that are nonviolent and acceptable to all, we can teach them to listen to different viewpoints. Preschoolers who have been shown how to solve problems compassionately and fairly will then respond with compassion when they see unfair situations.

Teacher, at circle time: Warren's mother brought some boxes for us to paint. She wants to help us make a mailbox for our post office. Who would like to help?

Children: (Several hands go up) Me! Me!

Teacher: Before we can start, there's a problem to solve. The art area is so crowded that Warren's mom can't get her wheelchair in.

Samantha, age four: That's not fair! (She and several other children run to the art area and start moving the furniture.)

Superhero play is a place where children can try out different ideas of fairness, both in the negotiation needed to set up the game, and in the play itself. Who decides what the game is? How do you decide who gets to play? Who chooses the roles? How rough will the play get? What happens if someone disagrees? How can you tell the good guys from the bad guys? What is the appropriate punishment for a monster or a bad guy? What about a player who won't follow the rules? Keeping the play fair for everyone grows increasingly important as group games get more complex. Children gradually learn that many games have set rules that help ensure fairness, and some, like sports, have referees to enforce the rules.

Big Questions: What Is Life and What Is Death?

"Playing dead" is one of the great traditions of children's play, and superhero play provides lots of opportunities for it. The definitions of *life* and *death* are not clear to children. How do you know when something is alive? Children look for clues based on what they can see and hear. Is something alive when it moves, such as rocks rolling down a hill, or a clock ticking, or the wind blowing? How about when it grows or changes, like the phases of the moon, or an image in a mirror? Is something dead when it is very still, like a sleeping dog, or a car when the engine is turned off? And what about dolls and puppets and characters on a TV program?

Most adults think they have a good sense of what is alive and what is dead, but like questions of right and wrong, different individuals and cultures give different answers to these questions. For preschoolers, the line between life and death is fluid and ambiguous. We should not be surprised when their questions about it show up in their play. The ideas they express about the subject while they play can be fascinating.

> *Did you know that Heaven is inside the Earth? It's a very happy place, with lots of miracles. It's called your morning afters, or your dead happiness, or your dead God. It's actually called your dead true. It means what happens to you in Heaven is true. Well actually, it's called your dead magic, your dead happiness magic.*
> —Charles, age three

Another set of questions comes up as children think about life and death. Where does new life come from, human babies in particular? What happens when you die? Maybe you come back to life.

> *When I get up from dying, I want to be Bambi.*
> —Vickie, age four

Does everything die? Will my parents die? Will I die? As with any exploration that they do, young children think out loud about these tricky issues through play, and superhero play is full of research opportunities.

Big Questions: What Is a Boy and What Is a Girl?

Preschoolers invariably become fascinated with gender and gender differences as older toddlers and explore them through play during the preschool years. They are intent on discovering how boys and girls are supposed to behave, and how they fit into that picture. Some children conduct this exploration very quietly, while some do it openly, with little regard for adult opinion. Superhero play is one of the many ways children experiment with their ideas about gender.

What knowledge does the typical preschooler bring to this play? Children in American culture are aware of gender categories before they are eighteen months old, because adults use the labels "boy" and "girl" often. Two-year-olds can usually identify their own gender. Around age three, children start making definitive statements about what they believe boys and girls can and cannot do. By four, many children prefer play-mates of their own gender, and show discomfort if a person's gender is not clear. They want to identify whether someone is male or female so they can know what to expect and how to respond.

Rob, age four: I'm Superman!

Anthony, age three: You can't be Superman, you're a girl.

Rob: I'm not a girl, I'm a boy.

Anthony: You are not.

Rob: (Getting angry) I am too.

Anthony: Uh-uh, you have long hair.

Rob: So? Boys can have long hair if they want.

Anthony: Yeah, but then you can't drive the bulldozer.

Rob: Can too! (Rob hits Anthony.)

Gradually, children become quite accurate in their ability to identify whether some-one from their own culture is a boy or a girl. That doesn't mean they understand what the words mean. The study of gender includes numerous overlapping and confusing questions. Am I a boy or a girl? What makes me a boy or a girl? How can I tell if other people are the same or different? What are boys and girls allowed to do, or not do?

How should I behave with people of my own gender, and with people of the opposite gender? Will my gender always stay the same, or can it change as I grow? How do boys and girls become men and women? What is the relationship between gender and sexuality? What does it mean to "be sexy," to "feel sexual," and to "have sex"? Why is sex so interesting to adults? Why do so many adults avoid talking about it directly?

We don't make it easy for children to find clear answers to these questions. Children's beliefs about gender identity, gender roles, and gender relationships are influenced by the religious, political, and cultural values that surround them, and in the United States, these influences often contradict each other. Some people have rigid definitions of male and female and the ways the sexes should relate, while others allow for variation and overlap. Most parents avoid discussing these issues with children, choosing to teach through ignoring, shaming, teasing, and exclusion. The most basic physical differences between females and males are kept covered. At the same time, sexuality is widely used in American culture as a way to get people's attention. The whole topic has an aura of excitement and danger—two of the elements children look for in superhero play.

Based on what they observe, preschoolers create elaborate rules about what boys and girls can do: Boys are strong. Girls should be sexy. Girls are afraid of monsters. Boys shouldn't be afraid of anything. Only boys can be leaders, use blasters, and wear Batman capes. Only girls can use magic wands, be witches or fairies, and wear dresses. They create these rules to make their complex world more predictable. They may state their beliefs very strongly, in the form of stereotypes, and embed them into their superhero roles and storylines. When different children's stereotypes disagree, as with Rob and Anthony in the scene above, they can become a source of conflict.

Telling children that they are wrong about their gender ideas and the way they play them out rarely changes their minds, because these beliefs do, in fact, accurately reflect their life experience and are based on the best thinking they can do. Unlike older children and adults, though, preschoolers are quite willing to change their stereotypes when given new experiences and information. Then they form a new opinion, and deny they ever believed the old one!

Big Questions: What Is Real and What Is Fantasy?

While infants and toddlers explore the world primarily through their senses, preschoolers must navigate another world as well—the world that opens through their imaginations. As their mental abilities expand, children develop inner lives that can be both exhilarating and confusing. As three-year-old Ariba said, "Listen! There are voices in my head. And they have special rules!"

Monsters, good guys, bad guys, ghosts, spirits, angels, and imaginary friends spring to life. Children strive to create clearer and more lifelike images in their minds, but the dividing line between reality and fantasy gets blurred. Re-creating these images in the physical world through superhero play is one way children can assert control over them and get a better sense of the boundaries.

But are the visions real? Are the feelings that go along with them real? Do others hear the same thoughts and see the same pictures? Is there a difference between using your imagination and telling a lie? How do people know what "real" is?

The answers children discover vary from culture to culture and family to family. Some people believe in angels, ghosts, and spirits, and some don't. Some take children's visions seriously, while some treat them as foolish baby talk. Every culture holds certain beliefs about what is real and what is fantasy, and one society's ideas about reality are considered a veil that hides the truth in another culture.

Children today have another factor that makes reality difficult to define. The ever more realistic special effects on TV and in movies have blurred what is possible and what is impossible. Can people fly? Many preschoolers believe the answer is yes. Can they change shape? Of course. Do dinosaurs roam the earth and eat people for breakfast? Yikes! And can people get punched, kicked, shot or electrocuted, crash their car, smash their head . . . and recover within seconds with no ill effects? Certainly. Just watch the *Home Alone* movies or professional wrestling to get your answer. In the past, most children were able to learn the difference between fantasy and reality without adult intervention, but today's children need a little help.

STORIES FROM THE CLASSROOM

Rico Rolls

If you observe a group of children playing superheroes, you'll find that they don't all have the same reasons for participating. Here's an example from my own classroom of how one child's interest sparked superhero play that touched on a variety of issues:

Rico, a three-year-old, was the youngest boy in the class. He spent much of his day in quiet pursuits, although I often saw him watching a group of four older boys play Spider-Man games as he drew or looked at books. One day, he made a discovery that changed the classroom. He took a plain, flat, boring sheet of paper, rolled it into a tube, pointed it at Peter, age four, and said, "Bang!"

Peter was one of the leaders of the superhero play, and he realized the importance of this invention immediately. He couldn't figure out how to roll the paper, but he wasn't very interested in learning. He wasn't worried, though. He walked up to Rico, put his head close and smiled. "You're my best friend, right?" he said, and Rico made him one.

Rico's social status soared. Peter invited him to make paper rolls for everyone and join the team. He was ecstatic. His mother commented that he was waking up early and begging to go to school.

The Spider-Man play up to that point had focused on flying, chasing, web climbing, and jumping from the "skyscrapers" that the children and staff designed out of mats and other portable climbing equipment. There were bad guys to trap, but they were all imaginary. Occasionally, participants used their fingers to shoot bullets, but Peter usually stopped them. "Spider-Man shoots webs," he said, and he showed his friends how to use their wrists to make the proper web-shooting motion.

Rico's paper rolls altered the equation. The game changed to killing bad guys. At first, the bad guys were imaginary, but that wasn't good enough for Peter. He started assigning the role to other children, but many of them refused. Then Dylan, age four, volunteered. For six weeks, Dylan had been focused on fighting and drawing scary, slimy aliens, an image he had gotten from a movie he had watched with his older brother. Now he showed he was fascinated with death. He said, "I'm dead. No, really, I'm really dead, I'm not just playing. Bad guys have to die. You can't see how dead I am, but God can. Only God knows what dead is, right?" He became the permanent bad guy, and convinced several friends to join him.

Meanwhile, others in the classroom had taken notice of Rico's invention. Jonah and Carlota were two four-year-old friends who loved all kinds of fantasy play, as long as it was physical. They could be mountain climbers, cooks, firefighters, and helicopter rescue pilots—all on the same day. They had recently started testing the classroom rules as part of their fantasy play, so the staff often had to intervene and help them find positive alternatives. They occasionally tried to join the Spider-Man play, but girls were not welcomed, even though the staff made it clear that Carlota could play any game that she wanted.

Jonah and Carlota studied Rico's design and quickly perfected the technique of rolling the paper. They announced that they were police officers from Chicago looking for burglars, and they crawled under all the furniture using the paper rolls as flashlights. At some point, they switched sides and became burglars, stealing and hiding puzzle pieces under chairs and behind shelves. They got upset when I stopped them, and insisted that the pieces were gold. I insisted that the pieces were, in fact, puzzle pieces that had to stay with the puzzles, but I gave them some gold-painted "treasure" rocks to use instead. They tucked their paper rolls in their pants, buried the rocks in the sandbox and wildly dug them up again with their hands, occasionally stopping to use their paper rolls as pirate walkie-talkies.

While Rico's paper roll idea spread through the classroom, he was busy improving the design. He was frustrated, because whenever he let go of the paper, it unrolled. So he experimented with tape, until he figured out how to hold the roll, tear the tape out of the dispenser, and apply it in the right place.

Peter never tried to use the tape. He said, "You're my best friend, right?" and Rico made him one. The next morning, Rico went straight to the art area and mass-produced the new model for all his Spider-Man friends.

Jonah and Carlota watched carefully, and within a short time they had adopted Rico's design. Their police game changed, because now they could throw their rolls repeatedly and use them as bombs. I stopped them from throwing them on the roof, and tried to set them up with bean bags and a target. Instead, they threw them, while on the run, into people's house games. When other children called them "bad," Jonah laughed and agreed, but Carlota was puzzled. She thought she was a good police officer who was killing bad guys. The two friends started to argue. They quickly resolved the problem by moving on to a new game— they became wolves and used the paper rolls as bones to chew on.

Rico still wasn't satisfied. He wanted his rolls to be tighter, so they wouldn't crush so easily. He tried various objects until he found that a fat pencil made a roll that was just right. He also discovered how to start rolling the paper in the corner, rather than the side, to make a longer version. He automatically made one for Peter.

Jonah and Carlota watched, then added hunting spears to their repertoire. I tied a hoop to a pole as a target, and made a new rule that the longer rolls couldn't be pointed at people. One Spider-Man, Roberto, age five, became fascinated with throwing his spear through the hoop from farther and farther distances. His interest spread, until we had to set up several hoops around the yard. He created a game where everyone ran full speed in circles and tried to throw paper rolls through the hoops. All the Spider-Mans joined the game and gave up killing bad guys for a few days.

Meanwhile, Rico stumbled on a new concept. He was trying to tape his roll when one end of it unraveled, leaving the roll in a wide cone shape. He taped it together that way and slipped it over his hand. He proudly showed his new invention to anyone who would pay attention.

Peter said, "You're my best friend, right?" But Rico said, "No!" Peter was stunned. He threatened to kick Rico out of the game, but Rico didn't seem to care. Peter begged the school's cook to make him one until she finally gave in.

Jonah and Carlota were delighted. They made their own cones, taped them on their fists, and called them laser guns.

Rico wasn't done. He wanted a longer roll. After several days of exploration, he learned how to make them supersized by putting one roll in the end of another, then stapling them together.

Peter tried to get one by bribing Rico with a roly-poly bug, but it didn't work. He pushed a chair over to the kitchen counter, looking for the cook.

It's clear in this story that superhero play fulfilled different needs for different children. For Rico, it was a way to explore his own resourcefulness and gain access to a powerful social group. Later, his part in providing the props for the play allowed him to challenge Peter's leadership. Peter was most interested in preserving that leadership role and maintaining his influence with his peers. Dylan was exploring his feelings and questions about death, while Roberto was testing his physical limits through the play. Jonah and Carlota were stretching their imaginations and bonding as friends, challenging adult rules along the way. All of them were exploring their own learning agendas, but all of them were united by their shared interest in superhero play.

CHAPTER 2

Understanding Adult Views on Superhero Play

"These superhero characters, I would never let them in my door. They're all about violence and anger and killing, and I don't want that in my house. I would never invite them over for dinner. So why should I let my grandson pretend to be one?"

—Marina, grandmother and caregiver of a four-year-old

SUPERHERO PLAY helps children understand who they are in the world and what it means to grow up. But many parents and teachers, like Marina, have doubts about letting children take part in it. This chapter will look at the following:

★ Why are caregivers worried about the media's influence on superhero play?
★ What are the behaviors children use in superhero play that concern caregivers?

Concerns about children's play are not new. They have been magnified in the United States, though, by living in a society where families and schools have very little control over the voices that compete for children's attention. Some of these influences, such as advertising, do not have children's welfare as their first priority. Many adults blame TV and other media for creating the problems or making them worse. Caregivers end up feeling that they have to hide their children from their own culture, a culture they often see as rude, obtrusive, and inhumane.

That's a sad state. Parents and teachers long for a world that will help them take care of children, but they feel under siege, instead. They have a long list of nightmares—gun violence, racism, kidnapping, environmental poisons, sexual exploitation, profanity, abuse—that are constantly reinforced and expanded by the evening news. Americans can't seem to agree on what is appropriate and what needs to change, we don't trust anyone to make the decisions for us, and we don't have the time to talk to each other and organize solutions. The world seems out of control.

One place where we believe we still have some control is with our young children. They are still dependent on us for their basic needs, so we can make a difference in how they view the world. It's a way we can stay hopeful and have a positive impact on the future.

Research does, in fact, support the importance of these early years in the formation of later abilities and attitudes. These studies have helped convince policymakers and schools to increase the availability of early education, institute anti-bias curriculum, and try to counteract the effects of poverty, neglect, and abuse as early as possible. But it has also added a sense of urgency to our desire to make a difference through our children. Many Americans are afraid that if children aren't sufficiently "grown up" by first grade, they will fall behind, fail, and get swept away by the worst aspects of the culture. Their worries cover everything from immediate safety concerns to their deepest fears for the future. Will our children be okay today? Will our world survive tomorrow?

When a child picks up a stick and shouts, "Bang! Bang!" those anxieties can turn to panic. All our nightmares seem to be coming true before our eyes. We want to know where our innocent babies learned to act like that. The first place many people focus blame is on TV. Before we look at the specific issues adults are concerned about, we have to look at how television, movies, and other media fit into the picture.

Why Are Caregivers Worried about the Media's Influence on Superhero Play?

Television gives children a miraculous window into the world, one that is far larger than families or schools could ever provide on their own. Still, many adults aren't sure they should allow their children access to that window. On the one hand, TV lets children learn about people and places that they would never experience on their own. It can teach facts and skills in ways that are exciting and fun. It can show the whole range of human emotions and responses. And it can be an ever ready babysitter when parents need to get dinner prepared, or when they just need a break. On the other hand, TV can model behavior that is hurtful, unrealistic, and self-destructive. It can sap children's imagination and energy, and instill desires for possessions they don't necessarily need. Here's how Bria, the mother of a three-year-old, expressed her ambivalence about TV:

> *She loves to watch TV. Even if I say no to it, she watches it at her dad's house, and at her grandparents'. I hate the constant fighting. I hate the commercials. I hate the way some of the girls act. How can she keep watching it? And if I sit down with her, I end up glued to it too. I really hate that.*

Many of the concerns parents and teachers express about children's TV center on "action" shows, including shows with superhero characters. These are programs that depend on a fast-moving pace and fighting to advance the plot. They may feature cartoon characters, real actors, or a combination of the two. They often use computerized special effects and trick photography. If you haven't watched children's TV lately, try this: Watch several children's superhero shows on TV, and pay attention to how your body feels.

I've given this assignment to many of my adult students. Some report that, during chase and battle scenes, they feel bombarded by sounds and images that send their heart rates soaring. Others say they get numb or hypnotized, and find it hard to look away from the screen. Certain images, like guns or people in danger, tighten their stomachs, necks, and chests. Some enjoy these feelings; others find them distressing or disorienting. They notice that they fall into the same "zombie state" they see on children: eyes wide, mouth slightly open, barely breathing, mind blank.

This is not an accident. Fast action video sequences, as well as many commercials, are edited to take advantage of a human biological quirk—feelings are faster than thoughts. Powerful emotions, such as anger, fear, and desire, spread quickly through our bodies and limit our ability to think clearly. Our senses go on high alert, and our bodies get ready to run or fight. Some of my students say they seek out this state, because it makes them feel more alive and "in the moment."

These reflex responses may be helpful in the face of danger, but TV and movie producers have learned to use them to their advantage. They leave exciting and often violent video images on the screen for only a few seconds, long enough to arouse children's feelings and catch their attention, but not long enough for children to think about what they are seeing. Before their minds have time to "kick in," the show moves on to the next image, often with a radical change in perspective, distance, color, or sound level, and they receive another dose of emotion and adrenalin. Each scene appears new, exciting, and a little bit dangerous. The pace may be reinforced by a soundtrack that includes a heavy, methodical beat. It's hard to turn away! Both TV and movies use these techniques, but TV shows and commercials rely on them more often, because they have to work harder to keep children from getting distracted by the outside world.

The belief among many television producers has been that young children can't understand plot and character development because their attention spans are too short. Adults who have spent hours reading picture books to children have always been skeptical of this claim, and recent research has supported them, showing that even very young children prefer to watch shows that have a sensible plot over video clips that are fast and flashy but have no story. Children's educational shows are now slowing down their pace and increasing the time of individual segments so that children can get to know characters better and think about what they are seeing.

Most children's action programs still rely on distressingly shallow plots and stereotyped characters, however, so they cover their shortcomings with sensory tricks: loud noises, bright colors, flashing lights, gross or scary images, wild special effects, and violent action. Sometimes this violence is slapstick (like the never ending disasters that befall Coyote as he chases Road Runner), but more often it's just confusing and senseless, with little connection to any humor, moral lesson, or happy ending.

Adrian, age four, and Jeremy, age three: We're Power Rangers!

Teacher: What do Power Rangers do?

Adrian: They kill people.

Jeremy: They kill monsters.

Adrian: They fight.

Jeremy: Yeah, they fight.

Teacher: Do they help people too?

Jeremy: No, they just fight.

Teacher: But at the end of the show, don't they talk about how to solve problems without fighting?

Adrian: Power Rangers just fight. Go, Go Power Rangers!

Media violence also tends to be sanitized. On screen, people punch each other, rub their chins, and walk away. In reality they would break bones in their hands and faces and would be unconscious or rolling on the floor in pain. On screen, vehicles crash at high speeds and villains shoot hundreds of bullets, then the heroes walk away with a few scratches. In reality, they and any number of innocent bystanders would be dead. These scenes are not included to help children think clearly about violence, but to keep them numb and watching.

Parents and teachers are particularly concerned about the weapons that appear in shows. Some children's superhero programs are nothing but a string of gun battles held together by a wisp of a plot, with characters that do little but kill monsters and blast away with oversized guns, tanks, and rockets. Guns are an easy way to finish a story segment, especially in the short formats used on most children's shows, because there is no need to spend time explaining what they represent: power and danger. Introducing a weapon or an explosion into a scene automatically makes it riveting and exciting. In the same way that adult programs and advertisements use sexuality to keep the audience watching, children's action shows rely on weapons and combat.

Most adults realize the media isn't responsible for all the problems they see in superhero play. They know that children were playing superhero and weapon games long before they watched TV. Still, many believe that TV shows, movies, and video games have made the problems harder to solve by using violence, stereotypes, rude behavior, and mind-numbing special effects just to keep children glued to the screen. They feel the media companies are taking advantage of children's interest in superheroes, not to help children grow, but to sell products. When adults talk about their reasons for disliking superhero play, media issues invariably play a part in every concern.

For more information on the effects of media on children, see the section in chapter 7 on "Sharing Information with Families about the Media."

What Behaviors during Superhero Play Concern Caregivers?

I have spoken to hundreds of parents and teachers about superhero play. Some have a long list of concerns about it; very few say they have none. Of those who are worried about the play, a majority would like to ban or severely restrict it. The behaviors children use in superhero play that concern caregivers include the following:

- ★ Hurting themselves and others
- ★ Relying on violence to solve problems
- ★ Reinforcing stereotypes
- ★ Restricting their imaginations
- ★ Disrupting routines and ignoring other learning opportunities

Hurting Themselves and Others

Keeping children physically and emotionally safe is a teacher's first duty. They know that preschoolers have a very tentative grasp of the difference between reality and fantasy, and that they often cannot predict the results of their actions or words. Superhero play, with its high energy and its focus on power and danger, can make the task of maintaining a safe classroom feel impossible. Here's how Lupe, the head teacher in a three- through five-year-old classroom, expressed it:

> *It's hard enough to keep these children safe. They don't understand what happens when your bike hits the wall, or when you throw a block in someone's face. They certainly don't understand what happens when you shoot a gun. When you add in superhero fantasies, especially with the kind of fights they see on TV, it's a wonder more children don't get hurt.*

Parents and teachers are right to be concerned about their children's physical safety during superhero play. Some of the moves children try to imitate are dangerous; young children have injured themselves and others flying off climbing structures, karate-chopping wood blocks, poking each other with pretend swords, and kicking so high that they land on their heads. With exciting images from the media in their minds as models, children can act with little understanding of the real-world consequences for themselves and others. Setting clear safety limits during play is essential to creating a classroom where children can learn, but children who believe they have superpowers can be difficult to control.

Caregivers know that feelings can get hurt as well. Many of us carry our own invisible wounds from insults we heard long ago. Some children take control of superhero play with strategies that are harmful, such as name-calling, exclusion, teasing, threats, and intimidation. Others hurt themselves by always taking passive and submissive roles in the play, even when they don't want to. Parents and teachers get upset when they see scenes like these:

Abe pushes Nathan under the climbing structure and says, "You have to be the bad guy or I'll knock your eyes out."

Michelle, Janis, Nancy, and Ophelia form a Powerpuff Girls team and bond with each other by roaming the playground, screaming out the rudest phrases they can imagine, harassing other children, and disrupting their play.

Robert doesn't let anyone tell him what to do. He tries to connect with a group of children playing castle by appointing himself king, but he destroys the play by insulting anyone who disagrees with him and trying to evict them from the game. He ends up with no one who will play with him. He shouts, "I hate everybody at this dumb school."

Joseph announces he is a wrestler named Joker. He walks around making fun of children, sometimes throwing them down and laughing hysterically in their faces.

Lisa will do anything to be included in the play. She accepts the role of Cruella DeVil even though she doesn't like it. She lets her playmates tell her what to do, including calling other children names and swearing at teachers. She mopes on the sidelines when others tease her, feeling alone and powerless.

Young children can learn a great deal about their place in the social scene if adults are available to guide these kinds of problems to more positive outcomes. It can be hard to provide this assistance, though, when children are deeply involved in superhero or villain characters, because some children believe that these roles give them permission to dominate or hurt people, or to command other children to do so.

Relying on Violence to Solve Problems

Parents and teachers worry about more than just the immediate safety problems associated with superhero play. They also worry about the long-term consequences of allowing children to include violence and weapons in their play. Many people fear that children will learn to view anyone who is different or disagrees with them as a monster, to be scorned, feared, and attacked. They are concerned that superhero play desensitizes children to other people's pain, and gives them a warped picture of how to handle feelings and solve problems. Some also dislike the play because they see it as the indoctrination of children into a gun-oriented, violent society.

We all bear images of school shootings in our minds, and struggle to understand how some children end up believing that guns are the best way to solve problems. Many of us also struggle to understand why some nations often use war for the same end. Among adults I have spoken to, the biggest fear is that children who focus on superhero play will grow into teens and adults who will become violent whenever they feel angry or unsafe. Even parents who believe strongly that they have the right to own and use guns have expressed concerns about the irresponsible use of weapons they see in superhero shows and in their children's play. They look at the newspaper headlines and wonder whether letting three-year-olds get involved with superheroes is the first step in turning them into murderers.

What place do weapons, especially guns, have in superhero play? Why do so many children want them? Recall that one of the reasons children get involved in superhero play is to explore powerful emotions. They do it by using roles, props, and actions that symbolize those desires and feelings and give children a way to understand and control them.

A gun is the most common symbol for fear and power in American culture. Most children see the image of a gun or hear about one from a peer every day, even if they have never seen a real gun in their entire lives. Guns are used freely in TV programs and movies and sold widely as toys. They are portrayed as the quickest way to feel powerful and solve problems. Newspapers and news shows highlight people who use weapons for crimes and wars. The gun control debate has been a hot-button topic in the United States for years. While young children may not be aware of the underlying issues in this argument, they pick up on the passionate debate. While children engage in mother and father role-play when they want to feel powerful within their families, when children turn their attentions to the larger world, nothing can compete with a gun as the symbol of power.

Here is how three-year-old Kane expressed his fascination with guns:

> *Old MacDonald had a gun, E-I-E-I-O*
> *With a gun gun gun, and a gun gun gun*
> *Here a gun, there a gun, everywhere a gun gun*
> *Pig has a gun*
> *Cow has a gun*
> *Horse has a gun*
> *I have a gun*
> *gun gun gun gun gun gun gun,*
> *gun gun gun gun gun*
> *Oh, yeah, I have an airplane too.*

Parents and teachers may understand that weapons play is a symbolic way to explore feelings, but they are worried that children are also imitating and practicing what the children see as adult behavior. Even if they have never witnessed violence in the real world, by sixth grade the average child has viewed 8,000 media murders. Many adults see a direct connection between the violence in society and the media and the violence that appears in superhero play. Many studies support this connection, showing that children who experience real-life violence or watch a lot of TV are more likely to be aggressive, desensitized to cruelty, and afraid they will be attacked. When young children see actual people or media characters repeatedly using violence to express power, they start to believe that violence is the accepted way to solve problems. However, while the link between watching violent shows and increased aggression (both immediate and long term) is clear from the latest research, it's also clear that most children who watch these shows and play war games don't become violent adults. Most learn that violence destroys friendships, and they look for better, more cooperative strategies when they are trying to balance power and friendships.

What about the few that don't? Some children use superhero play to control others through domination and fear. These are often the ones who have not yet developed good impulse control, are highly competitive, or who have been exposed to a lot of violence, either in their daily lives or through the media. Some of these children have been treated disrespectfully by older children or adults, and are anxious to take their turn on top; this mistreatment can take the form of physical violence, emotional abuse, unfair competition, or racism. Some have been exposed to videos filled with images that are far beyond their ability to understand. Some have witnessed violence in their homes and neighborhoods, and are trying to understand it by imitating it.

If these children become obsessed with a superhero character and are charismatic enough to become play leaders, their violent behavior can become the classroom norm. Keeping your classroom safe can be difficult when your top superheroes don't use their influence wisely. This is a situation where you may need to place severe restrictions on superhero play. See chapter 3, "Setting the Stage for Play," for further discussion on when to stop superhero play.

Reinforcing Stereotypes

Henry, age four, loved to play Superman and fight crime. One day, he said to his best friend, "Are you a Black? I don't like the Blacks, they're stupid. They're the bad guys."

Henry was confused. His best friend was African American, but he didn't seem to associate the term "Black" with his friend. He used the word as a label for the bad guys in his superhero play. By talking to his family and observing his play, which focused on putting robbers in jail, we realized that he was actually afraid of bank robbers, not African Americans. He had watched a TV show about bank robbers, and several of them wore black stocking caps. He had also heard an uncle make a racist comment that other adults felt bad about but never challenged. He fit these pieces together as best he could, and concluded "Black" meant "bank robber." Even though his intent was to understand right and wrong, he ended up with a damaging stereotype that he included in his play. The teachers were able to help him clarify his experience within a few days and he stopped the racist slurs, but how much damage had he done to his best friend's self-esteem?

A stereotype is a belief about someone based on that person's membership in a group, rather than the person's own behavior. It's not unusual for children to create these labels. They use them to simplify and sort the world, so they can understand it and make it predictable. The stereotypes they create on their own reflect their best thinking about their experiences. They often make these generalizations based on very little information, as four-year-old Isabel does with her reaction to her mother's occupation:

Isabel: Teacher, my mommy says she's a preschool teacher.

Me: That's right. She teaches at a different school.

Isabel: But she can't be a preschool teacher, she's a girl.

Me: Do you think that because I'm a boy?

Isabel: Yes. Preschool teachers have to be boys.

Such ideas are called pre-prejudices, and they can be changed with new experiences and information. In Isabel's case, I was the only preschool teacher she knew. It took about two weeks for her to change her ideas about teachers and gender, and then she proudly told everyone she met about her mother's occupation.

However, if pre-prejudices go unchallenged, or if they are actively reinforced by prejudiced adults, they can harden into long-lasting stereotypes. As children get older, they resist examining and changing these false beliefs, even in the face of contradictory evidence. When enough adults insist their stereotypes are fact, use them to make judgments about other people, and deny privileges and power to those people because of them, stereotypes lead to bias—racism, sexism, homophobia, and more.

Teachers who understand the anti-bias approach are aware that, while stereotypes may be a natural part of children's beginning thought process, they can negatively influence children's play. Stereotypes may seem to be about physical attributes such as skin colors and accents, but below the surface they are about which groups get to make decisions, which get to tell others what to do, and which are labeled good and bad. One of the ways society passes those stereotypes on to children is to represent oppressed groups as alien, abnormal, weak, bad, or not human, while showing the dominant group as normal and good. Superhero play is particularly susceptible to bias, because it explores questions of who has power and who is good, and it often involves rejecting or killing characters who embody evil. Children build their superhero roles— good guys, bad guys, and victims—around these ideas. While they are only trying to play out their own feelings of strength and inadequacy, it's no surprise that they often borrow from society's stereotypes when they decide what the roles should look like.

Some caregivers are particularly sensitive to the way media characters can reinforce racism. While few writers and producers would knowingly use racist stereotypes, action shows sometimes use characters, particularly villains, which children interpret in ways that reinforce those stereotypes. A dark, disfigured, or foreign-looking character, combined with sinister music, makes a convenient bad guy. In the same way that a gun is a quick plot device to create suspense, a dark villain with an accent provides writers an easy character that children will interpret as dangerous and evil. Even when the characters are not meant to be African American, Middle Eastern, or Asian, such roles depend on stereotypes for their effect. Try this: the next time you see a dark cartoon villain, imagine the character is a blond woman in an angel costume. Does the character still have the same visual impact? When children combine what they see on TV or in movies with other images they absorb in American culture, they can unconsciously form racial and ethnic stereotypes.

Racism is one major concern of caregivers. Gender stereotypes are another. For many children, the bravery, strength, physical skill, competitiveness, leadership, emotional control, and aggression displayed by action heroes are male traits. That doesn't mean that girls don't display these qualities, but they are seen as "acting like boys" when they do. By early elementary school, adults and peers express disapproval by calling them tomboys. Similarly, the helplessness and emotionality children display in victim roles and the cooperation seen in housekeeping play are labeled as feminine, and boys who show these traits may be teased and called sissies, wimps, fags, or girls. As is typical with stereotypes, those who don't conform to them are seen as deviants, rather than proof that the stereotypes are wrong. Without some adult guidance, superhero play can become a place where children are forced to conform to rigid gender divisions, avoid exploring gender roles, and view women as less important than men.

Gender stereotypes are common in the media. Despite efforts to present a broader view of male and female behavior on some shows, many shows still reinforce the worst kinds of gender stereotyping. A helpless, pretty girl in a victim role is easier to use then a helpless boy, because there is no surprise in seeing her in that role. In one study, three-quarters of children between ages ten and seventeen described the men on TV as violent, and two-thirds said the men were usually angry. Many of them said they saw women helping their families on TV, but not men. When the media reinforce these gender stereotypes, and they are not challenged by what children experience in the world, children grow up believing that men and women can behave in only limited ways.

Another group that doesn't fare well in the media is fat people. For example, the original Power Rangers used a moronic fat character who stuffed food in his mouth and crashed into the scenery, supporting a cultural stereotype about people who are large. While the producers may want children to get the message that it is foolish to act like that, children also get another message: you don't want to look like that. The message that skinny is best is reinforced throughout the media, not just on children's television.

Fool, bully, witch, stepmother, monster, magician, warrior—these are images that, like violence, occur throughout literature. When used well, they are archetypes that help children understand complex human characters. In mediocre stories and television programs, they only serve to reinforce and perpetuate the racism, sexism, and other biases that many parents and educators are trying to counteract.

Restricting Their Imaginations

Many parents and teachers watch their children's imaginations blossom with great joy and pride. Scenes like this one dismay them:

> *Frederick, age three: I'm an orange Power Ranger!*
>
> *Sam, age five: You can't be an orange Power Ranger. There is no orange Power Ranger.*
>
> *Frederick: Why not?*
>
> *Sam: It's not on TV. You can't just make one up.*

Parents and teachers don't like seeing children abandon their own ideas and adopt characters and stories from the media as the sole basis for their superhero play. They are particularly upset when their children say they can't play a game without the toys and clothing advertised on TV. Why do children decide that these images are better than their own—bigger, stronger, more grown up, and more real?

This change in fantasy play often coincides with a shift in children's focus from exploring the world on their own to developing friendships. Preschoolers discover that the best way to play out their increasingly complex fantasies is to do it with friends, which limits what fantasy images they can use. Unless the child who leads the play is particularly strong willed or charismatic, ideas that are eccentric or unique are difficult for everyone in the group to follow. When the goal is to create friendships, too many surprises can threaten group cohesion. Children who are being creative can be shut out of the play if their ideas stray too far from what the others understand. Many preschoolers start using conformity as a sign of friendship at this stage: If you want to play, you have to play the game the right way. Familiar characters and stories make the job much easier.

In the past, oral myths and stories provided these images for children. Today, they often come from the media. TV images are much more complete and grown-up looking than anything young children could create, so most readily adopt them. Children who haven't seen the shows quickly fall in line so they won't be left out. If children are playing a game based on a TV show they have all watched, others will try to watch that show if they want to join in. While parents are trying to hold on to the past, children are looking for the best way to move into the future, and that future centers on their friends.

Toys and clothing that feature commercial images make superhero characters even more compelling. The repetitive advertising and limited play value of many superhero toys helps reinforce the idea that there is only one right way to play the game.

> *Emil, age four: Do you have a Pokemon egg?*
>
> *Julianna, age four: No.*
>
> *Emil: Then you can't play this game.*
>
> *Juliana: Why not?*
>
> *Emil: Only these eggs can give you the right power. You have to open them just right, like this. Ask your momma to buy you one.*
>
> *Juliana: Okay.*

Take a look at the commercials on TV through a young child's eyes. They appeal to children by supporting the need to feel powerful and valued by their peers. They tap into their desires by showing children who are smart, strong, popular, beautiful, brave, and in charge—in other words, children who have taken over the grown-ups' role. The products themselves are given magical qualities through animation and trick photography.

Programs and commercials exist to sell products, but children are naïve about this. Money can be made by convincing children that their happiness depends on having the toys, food, and clothing shown on TV. Some children's cartoons are really half-hour-long sales pitches. The goal of many commercials is not only to sell specific products, but to instill brand awareness and loyalty in children as early as possible. Adults worry that children believe these products will fulfill their needs. (Are adults any different when they buy cars based on the good times shown in car commercials?) They know that many of the toys are almost useless without the additional accessories promoted in the same commercials. They see the deception continuing in the toy stores, where the packaging often makes promises that the products can't possibly keep. When toys fail to deliver, or when children don't get what they want, parents know they will be left to get the blame and pick up the pieces. Manufacturers, advertisers, and store managers aren't the ones who have to deal with the tantrums.

Here is what some parents had to say about their children's response to commercials:

"I don't know what to do. He wants whatever he sees on TV. They make the stuff seem so exciting. Even if I say no, he keeps at it until somebody buys it for him. But then he needs to buy something else to make it work like on the commercials. More, more, more. That's what it's all about, isn't it?"
—*Isis, mother of a four-year-old*

"When I say no to buying a toy, she has a tantrum, right there in the store. I wish I could make the store manager deal with it. And the toy manufacturers, and the advertisers. It's such a setup. And how is she supposed to feel proud of her family when all she knows is that we're too poor to keep up?"
—*Gary, father of a three-year-old*

"He used to be a different character every week—a cat, or a dragon, or a wizard. I never knew who I was going to find in my house in the morning. We would make costumes out of anything. Now he's obsessed with Spider-Man. He wants to wear his Spider-Man pajamas all day. He wants every Spider-Man toy he sees. If it's homemade, it doesn't work for him. That's baby stuff, now." —*Sara, mother of a five-year-old*

Disrupting Routines and Ignoring Other Learning Opportunities

For some teachers, superhero play would be acceptable if children kept it safe and confined it to the playground. But there are children who get so obsessed with the play that they refuse to abandon their characters, no matter what time of day. As Rondelle, a teacher in a three-year-old classroom, put it, "How am I supposed to run a circle time or an art project when all these kids want to do is run around and shoot each other? I can't get them to stop." The high energy of most superhero play doesn't fit in well with organized lessons or quiet meals and naps. It not only stops the superheroes from learning, it makes it difficult for other children to participate.

In my observations, children have a hard time stepping out of superhero play to take part in other activities for the following reasons:

★ They are insecure in their friendships, and worry that they will lose them if they don't constantly connect with their peers.
★ They want to test adult authority.

★ They are focused on fearful images that they can't get out of their minds.

★ They are having fun, and see the other curriculum as boring.

These needs are particularly difficult for teachers to handle in the middle of transitions and organized activities.

Another way children disrupt the classroom is by using every item in the classroom as a superhero play prop. I once observed a classroom where a group of children was running through the playground shooting at each other. The objects they were using for weapons included a plastic pear, a puzzle piece, a crayon, and a baby bottle. All had been taken from indoor curriculum areas, and all ended up tossed aside in the sand or inside children's pockets. The opportunity for children to participate in other planned activities was reduced, and some of the equipment was in danger of being ruined. I have seen projects completely trashed by children who decided that they had to have one special piece of the setup for their guns.

Play also becomes diminished when children believe they can use every space in the classroom and on the playground for superhero play. Quieter, more reflective activities get swept away, and children feel intimidated. The only game left to play is the superhero game.

STORIES FROM THE CLASSROOM

Frames

A kindergarten teacher at one of the local elementary schools called me and asked for help. She reported that her playground, which she shared with two other classes, was being overrun by Superbad Spaceboys, a wild game of chase, soldiers, martial arts, and imaginary weapons. The Spaceboys were even starting to play out their roles inside the classrooms. While no one had gotten hurt, the teachers were concerned about the intimidation of the other children and the disruption of the classroom routines. The teachers mentioned one name repeatedly: Gerald.

I arrived to observe the playground early in the morning, with notepad, pencil, and tape recorder. I wanted to sketch out the playground before the children arrived. It was a typical setup for a public elementary school, designed as a place to let out excess energy between lessons, rather than a part of the classroom. There was a multicolored climbing structure, a small lawn, and a concrete patio with tables and benches. It had one unusually large oak tree that provided shade and an interesting play space around it.

The yard was eerily quiet at 7:30 A.M. I imagined that the tree, the grass, and the climber were all meditating, preparing for the morning's onslaught. School started at 8:30, but children were dropped off as early as 7:45. The teachers were expected to get ready for their day while somehow keeping an eye on the outdoors. In reality, they told me that the yard went mostly unsupervised. An aide would walk out every ten minutes or so to dispense time-outs and make sure no one required medical attention.

I was the first to find the rusty bed frames. They lay in a tangle of bars and wheels and springs at the edge of the playground, at least three sets in all. Some good citizen had backed up their vehicle to the fence in the middle of the night, tossed them over, and disappeared. Now they were somebody else's problem.

I pointed out the stack of junk to a teacher. She passed the message to the janitor, but the pile was still there when the first children drifted in. They gathered around it, surprised, intrigued, and a little suspicious. They asked each other questions and speculated about its history, but no one touched it. By 7:50, a group of six boys and girls were standing in a rough semicircle ten feet away.

A girl named Elise was the first to break the spell. She walked over and carefully pulled a bar out of the heap until it lay flat on the ground. The others immediately set to work, until all the parts were laid out in a pattern of rectangles and triangles about ten feet long and six feet wide. The children then methodically investigated all the physical possibilities of the frames. Some worked on their own, some in small groups. They jumped over the bars in zigzag patterns, balanced on them, picked them up to feel their weight, spun the wheels as fast as they could, and gingerly sat on the springs and bounced. They talked quietly and seriously to each other, except for an occasional burst of excitement when someone discovered a new use for a frame piece. Every few minutes, an aide would appear to tell the children to move away. They would retreat into a semi-circle until the adult disappeared, then wait for Elise to lead them back to their work.

After ten minutes of this exploration, a new boy entered the game. He called out, "Superbad!" and jumped and twirled over a bar. Another boy imitated him and made a blaster sound.

Elise reacted quickly. "No!" she said. "No Spaceboys in this house. This is the safe house." She began organizing the game, naming the spaces created by the frame pieces as rooms in a house and assigning roles to children. There were bedrooms for sleeping babies and a living room for the whole family. The bedsprings became puppy beds, and several cooks were told to set up a pretend kitchen behind the nearby oak tree. As each new child entered the yard and came over to see what was going on, Elise gave them a place and a role, then negotiated with anyone who didn't like the assignment. She let several children make up their own roles, but there were two roles they were not allowed to choose: Superbad Spaceboy and Mother. Anyone who insisted they were a Superbad Space-boy was banished to the climber, and there was only one Mother, and that was Elise.

By 8:05 about twenty children were in the yard, and twelve of them were participating in the house game. Three Superbad Spaceboys scaled the climbing structure and jumped off repeatedly, using a variety of twirls, kicks, and shouts. They tried their best to looked puffed up and aggres-sive, but their game seemed harmless.

Suddenly, one of them cried, "Gerald." A wiry, brown-haired boy came through the gate at full speed. He waved at the Superbad Spaceboys, but headed for the bed frames.

"Hey, guys, what's that?" he yelled. "A spaceship?"

Everyone looked to Elise. "No way," she said, and she turned away with her nose up. "It's a house. You can be the daddy."

"No way," said Gerald. "Come on men, let's go!"

Two of Elise's prized puppies took off and followed Gerald to the climbing structure, shouting, "Hee-yah!" and karate chopping the air. Two other boys who had been playing elsewhere joined them.

"Stupid puppies. Run away, I don't care," Elise shouted.

"We're not puppies no more," said one. "We're Superbads! Hee-yah!"

Eight Superbad Spaceboys gathered under the climber. Elise moved nervously from room to room, calming her children while preparing them for an attack. "Don't worry babies, go back to sleep. Momma's gonna keep you safe from those bad guys."

They didn't have to wait long. Gerald and the Superbad Spaceboys came screaming and jumping across the yard. They ran in circles around the bed-frame home with guns blazing. Elise shouted and waved her hands. Some of her offspring imitated her, while others whined. One cowered with her head on her knees. She looked like she was praying.

The aide appeared and added her voice to the confusion. "Gerald! You stop! All of you boys take a time-out! Elise, get away from that junk! You'll hurt yourself!" She waited until her orders were followed before going back inside.

Elise and her family gathered under the tree. The Superbad Spaceboys sat on the time-out benches, whispering and making plans.

Elise walked over to Gerald. "I don't want you shooting my babies," she said.

"They're a bunch of stupid scaredy-cats," he replied.

"They need their sleep. Come over and I'll make you a spaceship next door."

The aide stuck her head out of the door. "Don't talk to them, they're on time-out. Ten more minutes to morning meeting!"

More and more children entered the yard. Almost every one of them paused to size up the situation, then joined one of four groups: Gerald's benched Superbad Spaceboys, Elise's baby and puppy house, a group of foursquare players on the patio, or a group of children who seemed to be avoiding the conflict by wandering aimlessly.

Elise reclaimed her house, but she had lost several followers. She actively recruited more from the wanderers, who either shook their heads and looked away or beamed as if they had been blessed and joined her game. Once she had babies and puppies in every room, she called them to attention.

"Okay, everybody, we have to make a new house. We gotta make room for a spaceship." She moved some of the bed-frame pieces to create an area that extended to the tree. She looked over at the Superbad Spaceboys, now a group of eleven. "Hey Gerald, I'm making you guys a spaceship with no babies." Gerald turned his back toward her, muttering insults, but the rest of his gang kept glancing over.

A minute later, Gerald decided the time-out was finished. "Let's go!" he shouted, and he led his troops back to the climber. Some of them hesitated.

"Come on, breakfast is ready," said Elise. "Bad guy breakfast. It's a spaceship restaurant."

A few of the Superbad Spaceboys walked over. Gerald quickly intercepted them. "Guys, this ain't a restaurant," he said.

"Yes it is," said Elise. "It's got drinks with energy vitamins and stuff."

"We don't eat that stuff, that's for babies. We only eat moon rocks," said Gerald.

"We got moon rocks. Come on, here are some moon rocks." She held out her empty hands.

Gerald stepped into the spaceship room. He pretended to grab the moon rocks from her and wolf them down. The rest of the Superbad Spaceboys imitated him. His three most trusted lieutenants got to sit with him in the spaceship, while the others spread out under the tree and along the fence, waiting to be served by the babies and puppies.

"Watch out, babies," said Elise. "These are some mean bad guys, and they got no manners."

"That's right," growled Gerald.

"That's right! No manners!" growled some of the Superbad Spaceboys as they devoured their moon rocks.

The aide stepped outside again. "I told you to stay away from that. Time for morning meeting." She rang a bell, and most of the children hurried inside.

Gerald, Elise, and three Spaceboys didn't move. The aide stuck her head out again. "Morning meeting. Inside. Now." The rest of Elise and Gerald's followers ran for the door. The two leaders hesitated and looked at each other. Elise shrugged and walked across the lawn. Gerald followed slowly, looking glumly at his feet.

I spent the next half hour talking to one of the aides about my recommendations:

- Assign at least one aide to supervise the yard at all times, with clear rules and consequences that all the teachers agree on.

- Provide safe materials, like blankets and large outdoor blocks, that the children could move around and build with.

- Incorporate the children's fantasy play stories into the literacy curriculum.

- Add more large motor challenges to the yard and change them regularly.

- Acknowledge Elise's and Gerald's leadership when they used their influence in a positive way.

My ideas received a polite but cool reception—they included too much that was not part of the budget and not part of the job. "I'll talk to the teachers, and we'll see," said the aide. I agreed to write up a report.

I walked to my car and heard the sound of metal being tossed into a dumpster. As I drove away, I could see a couple of metal bars peeking over the edge of the bin, wheels pointing toward the playground, back to the girls and boys who, for a short time, had given them life.

The staff's concerns were typical for teachers who were dealing with superheroes in their classroom. They were worried about the physical and emotional safety of the children, about the disruption of their routines, and about the long-term effects of the violence and weaponry that seemed to bond the Superbad Spaceboys. All of these concerns were valid, but they wanted to solve the problems by magically making the play go away. Instead, they needed to find ways to support the children who were involved by including their ideas in the curriculum, while taking the time to set clear, consistent limits on the negative behavior. They didn't believe their jobs required or allowed that. The problems were certain to continue, and I feared that some of the class leaders were destined to be labeled "bad boys."

CHAPTER 3

Setting the Stage for Play

"I get very con-
fused about
what to do
about super-
hero play.
Do I stop it?
Let it go? On
the one hand,
it seems so
important to some of the children in
my class. They want to do it every day.
On the other hand, once it gets started
it takes over. It's like a tornado in my
classroom, it destroys everything in
its path."

—Sergio, teacher in a four-year-old classroom

MANY CHILDREN love superhero play. Many teachers, like Sergio, have serious concerns about the play and want to stop it. Caregivers feel justified in ignoring children's desires and prohibiting the play because they see it as unsafe, both short and long term. Children feel justified in ignoring adults' fears because the play helps them explore so many important questions, and they don't understand why they should stop. Two groups of people, two different points of view. In many ways, this is a cross-cultural conflict between adult culture and child culture, and it should be handled with the same respectful attitude with which we handle cross-cultural conflicts with families.

Teachers don't like to support superhero play because they feel it opens the door to danger, conflict, and chaos. That's always a possibility when you pay attention to children's fantasies—the image of early childhood as always sweet and peaceful is a myth! But refusing to acknowledge children's fantasies and feelings won't make them disappear. Teachers who try to steer clear of superhero play are often unprepared when it suddenly takes over their classrooms.

You can support and welcome the drama without letting it run the show, and you can do it in ways that allow both children and adults to feel their opinions are respected. This chapter looks at strategies you can use to set the stage for positive superhero play when it appears, including these:

* Reflecting on your own attitudes about superhero play
* Setting clear, respectful limits
* Using children's healthy impulses to redirect their play
* Helping children become more aware of safety
* Negotiating with children about their ideas
* Knowing when to stop superhero play

Reflecting on Your Own Attitudes about Superhero Play

Before you can get ready for superhero play, it's useful to examine your beliefs about it. What are the aspects of the play that you appreciate? What are you concerned about? Some teachers enjoy the play, but don't make any effort to plan for it. Some would like to respect children's desire to play superheroes, but are too worried to let it happen in their classrooms. Some tolerate the play, but would rather avoid it. Many think of it as a hindrance to their curriculum, and want to suppress it.

A majority of teachers I have spoken to have tried one of two ways to resolve the superhero play conflict: ignore the play and just let it happen, or place severe restrictions on it, sometimes even banning it. Both approaches can have unintended consequences.

Ignoring superhero play tells children that the best answers to their questions come from the culture around them, including the media, and that their interests are not worth including in the curriculum. Banning the play tells children the adult point of view is the only one that counts, and their questions are too uncomfortable to discuss. In my experience, neither of these approaches works well. I recommend that teachers welcome the play into their curriculum and plan for it. That way, children can see their ideas are respected, while families and staff can see that the play will be kept safe and reflect values they can support.

Some people advocate standing back and letting children's play unfold on its own with as little adult guidance as possible. They think that adults should intervene only when there is a clear and immediate safety problem that the children can't resolve. They believe that if teachers set up a safe environment and stand back, children will work out their relationships and feelings on their own.

I'm certainly sympathetic to this view. Play can teach, heal, and promote growth, and when it is working well, it shouldn't be disturbed. But a completely hands-off approach ignores how culture can shape children's superhero play and contradict the positive values we want them to learn. Children hurt each other when they play out the oppressive and violent strategies for gaining power they see around them. While preschoolers' imaginations may have grown tremendously, they are still not able to envision alternative approaches without adult help. When adults choose not to intervene, children assume that adults approve of oppression and violence. Ignoring the play may avoid conflict, but it doesn't help children find solid answers to the deeper questions they are asking.

What about banning the play altogether? One reason adults stop superhero play is to keep children safe, both immediately and in the future. Safety has to be a first concern for teachers, and there are certainly times when we have to use our adult knowledge and power to make decisions about safety, even if that means ignoring what children want. Children don't get to run out in the street or throw toys in their friends' faces just because they feel like it. Sometimes teachers must put restrictions on superhero play, or even ban it, to keep their classrooms safe.

But the idea of keeping children safe can be misused. Teachers sometimes talk about safety when what they really mean is that superhero play is too noisy, messy, or active, or it doesn't fit with their curriculum plans. Or they can get caught up in worries about possible future problems, such as the game getting out of hand, a child being mistreated, or the children becoming violent as teenagers, while forgetting to look at what is actually happening to children in the moment. Teachers can also be anxious about what families think ("Parents will be mad at me if I let this continue") and parents can worry about what teachers think ("Will my child become the class problem?").

These feelings shouldn't be ignored. However, they call for thoughtful planning and dialogue with families and children, not eliminating superhero play. Banning the play may relieve adult fears, but it creates a problem when children are confused about why it's been done, as these two children were:

> *Teacher: Baija, it looks like you want to play [a Superman chase game].*
>
> *Baija, age three: My Mommy says, "No."*
>
> *Mika, age five: Why?*
>
> *Baija: It's too scary.*
>
> *Mika: If you have too much fun, grown-ups don't like that.*
>
> *Baija: Why?*
>
> *Mika: (Shrugs shoulders and joins the game.)*
>
> *Baija: (Shrugs shoulders and sighs, then runs to catch up.)*

Banning superhero play can backfire and make the play even more attractive, increasing the risky behavior teachers are trying to discourage. Exploring power, independence, and fairness are all reasons children get involved in the play. When children see adult rules as oppressive and unfair, they have an even greater need to play out their feelings through weapons and superheroes. Adults find themselves in a spiral of conflict with children, imposing more and more restrictions while the children look for more and more ways to challenge or sneak around rules. Superhero play is one of the first places that young children systematically lie, sneak, ignore, and bend rules to get what they want. ("This isn't really a gun, it's just a power drill that spits out bolts," said one four-year-old.) For many modern American children, the drive for autonomy is stronger than any guilt, shame, or worry adults try to load on them.

When teachers deny children the power to choose their own play, and the restrictions make little sense to them, children learn that the biggest person gets to make the rules regardless of whether the rules are fair. That may work with young toddlers, who can't imagine any other rules, but four-year-olds can become skeptical and think of the rules as irrational and disrespectful. They start to see adults as obstacles to learning, rather than allies. That may be how much of the world works, but it's not what I want children to learn within my classroom community.

Even when young children are willing to follow the rules at home or in the classroom, many parents and teachers have discovered that severe restrictions give only a temporary illusion of control. As soon as children are old enough to be alone with their peers, they usually can't resist participating in fantasy games that are so full of energy, excitement, and friendship. Parents find that, unless they isolate their children, their attempts to keep superheroes and weapons at bay are doomed.

Banning superhero play can also create confusion for children about one of the big questions they are trying to answer—what is real and what is fantasy? When teachers refuse to acknowledge the difference between actual violence and symbolic violence by banning both, they are missing an important opportunity to help children understand the difference.

Keep in mind that understanding and controlling fear and other strong emotions is central to superhero play, and children do it symbolically by fighting monsters and villains. Superhero fantasies can be disturbing to adults, but pretending to kill space creatures by shooting them and slicing off their heads with magic swords is not actually dangerous. Unless the children who are playing out this scene are being reckless, there is no need to stop them. An exchange between Tanya and her six-year-old son, Peter, shows how confusing this can be for adults:

> *Tanya: I tell him he can't play with guns, but he takes a bite out of his toast and starts shooting with it. I get scared. I just don't want him to grow up thinking it's okay to kill anything that gets in his way.*

> *Peter: But Mom, I'm not hurting anybody. Don't you know it's just pretend?*

On the other hand, attacking another child because she won't play the game is dangerous, and should be stopped. That's when teachers can bring up some of their adult concerns and help children separate fantasy from reality. While it may seem contradictory to some people, when we allow children to participate in safe but seemingly violent superhero play while firmly stopping truly dangerous behavior, it helps them learn to express feelings and solve real problems safely.

Ignoring or banning superhero play eliminates opportunities for teachers to help children find positive answers to their most passionate questions. They leave children with the perception that their questions are trivial, wrong, or even dangerous. Fortunately, there are several ways to start supporting the play so it can succeed in the classroom. Some of these strategies work best when they are implemented before superhero play even shows up.

Setting Clear, Respectful Limits

Even the most carefully planned environment can be misunderstood or tested by children. They may destroy the cardboard box the staff brought in for a spaceship. They may dump sand and leaf potions in the middle of the reading area. One child may try to get another to follow her ideas through intimidation and threats. While teachers should always strive to support and enrich children's play ideas, they also have to keep their classrooms physically and emotionally safe. It's difficult for children or their families to feel part of a classroom community when their basic need for safety isn't met. Teachers must create limits, expectations, and consequences that are age appropriate, clear, firm, and fair. Children can thrive when they all know that the teachers are doing their job.

Well-established rules are particularly important for young superheroes, because their play can be loud, fast, and physical. Players can get hurt when they believe they have superpowers, and other children can get flattened when four- and five-year-olds are being "bad guys." It's much easier to establish your safety rules before these games appear, when children are doing other highly active play like car racing, horses, and firefighters. In fact, I make a point of setting up these kinds of games near the beginning of the year to help me introduce these rules. Then everyone will know what you mean when you have to stop a pack of Evel Knievels from riding their trikes up the slide, or when you have to remind a team of Incredible Hulks that they can squeeze mats and pillows, but not people. The more children can learn beforehand about staying safe, getting help from adults when they need it, and negotiating with each other about their play ideas, the simpler it will be to keep superhero play within bounds. These are good skills for children to have in all kinds of play situations.

Children need clear rules about physically unsafe behavior, but they also need rules about other hurtful actions. When young children use threats, ethnic slurs, name-calling, intimidation, exclusion, or coercion as part of superhero play, they don't always understand the full meaning of their words, but they do understand that words have the power to hurt. Adults must react quickly to help children express what they want in positive ways, before insults become an accepted part of their classroom culture.

Creating clear boundaries on psychologically unsafe behavior can be tricky for many adults. The awkward strategies young children use to gain power and friendship during superhero play can bring up memories of our own emotional scars inflicted by peers in the past. Teachers can overreact in these situations and become punitive in their discipline. For example, as a beginning teacher I was unable to help children I labeled as bullies because of my own childhood experiences with bullies. I thought I was protecting the victims by punishing the bullies, but I was really just expressing my own childhood anger at feeling powerless. I did little to help any of them feel powerful in a positive way. When I could finally look past my labels and support all the children's needs, I was more successful in setting firm but fair boundaries and changing the behaviors of both groups.

I have found that when teachers have a strong emotional response to children's behavior, they can often connect it to feelings about past mistreatment of themselves or their families. By becoming more aware of their own histories and beliefs, teachers can stay focused on the children's experiences and see all of them as fully human. Then they are more able to set limits that provide positive guidance.

In many schools, safety restrictions and rules become a long list of unacceptable behaviors, with punishments for children who disregard them. But rules have to be more than that if we want to use them to facilitate play rather than silence children. Rules should help children understand how to get what they want in acceptable ways. They should include the following:

★ Where and when activities are allowed ("You can play your chase games outside after circle time.")

★ What children can do if someone is treating them unfairly ("If you don't want to play, put out your hand and say, 'Stop! I don't want to play that game!'")

★ What happens when a rule is broken ("If people tell you to stop shooting at them and you won't stop, a teacher will help you find another game to play.")

★ How to resolve conflicts without resorting to violence ("I won't let you solve this problem by threatening him. Do you have any ideas for something you both can say yes to?")

What boundaries help superhero play happen safely? Aside from limits on behaviors that are clearly dangerous, you may need to regulate the time, place, or materials that can be used. Time restrictions are particularly helpful when older children are mixed with younger ones for part of the day, such as when kindergarten or afternoon school-age children are in the same yard as preschoolers. Play that works for five- and six-year-olds may be dangerous for two- and three-year-olds. Even when the older children are trying to be safe they can scare younger children, because the "littles" can't tell they are just pretending. The two- and three-year-olds end up plastered against the fences, afraid to play their own games. Is there a time when the older children can have the play-ground or dramatic play area to themselves? If children's fantasies create a fearful atmosphere in the classroom for those who aren't part of the game, you may want to limit the play to particular times of the day when the groups can play separately.

Schools frequently restrict the place where superhero play can happen, as well, usually to the outdoors. Too often, though, teachers do this to avoid including super-hero play in their curriculum. Limiting where children can play works well when children are given adequate time outdoors, activity zones are clearly defined so the play won't interfere with other games, and curriculum plans support the play.

Some teachers have set aside areas exclusively for superhero play, around a climbing structure, in a playhouse, on a lawn, or in a new area delineated with portable room dividers, safety cones, or even yellow construction tape. This happens most often when a few children are attached to a superhero game, but there are other children who have different ideas for large motor play. For example, one teacher used chairs and dividers to make a temporary weapons zone in one corner of her playground; children who were previously intimidated by sword and gun fighting then felt safe to play their own games on the rest of the yard. The boundaries of such areas need to be clearly defined, because children in the middle of fantasy play don't remember invisible lines.

Limitations on materials are also widespread in preschool classrooms. The most common are restrictions on what can be used as guns, swords, and bombs. Young children can turn practically anything into a fantasy weapon. While teachers like to see children use equipment in new and creative ways, they get frustrated when everything they have carefully prepared for a project gets turned into weapons. Other children can get upset as well, because they never get to explore the materials.

In many schools that I visit, teachers are unclear about whether they should step in to stop this use of materials. There is nothing wrong with requiring that crayons be used for drawing, pinecones stay by the science table, and puzzle pieces stay with their puzzle frames, as long as you can direct children to supplies that can be used for their games. There is also nothing wrong with making judgments about what is safe to use—I don't let children run around swinging long, four-unit blocks or brandishing broomsticks, because the potential for injury is too high. Not everything in the classroom needs to be available as a superhero resource.

However, certain materials seem to fall into a gray zone. Can small blocks and other construction materials be used to make weapons? How about art supplies? Can they go outside? Can children keep them in their pockets and cubbies? Preschoolers become very interested in these unclear boundaries as part of their exploration of power. They test out the rules and work around them by claiming they've made skyscrapers, rocket ships, or fire hoses, even though their constructions look and sound suspiciously like guns. The small manipulative shelves are where children often choose to find out exactly how serious adults are about their weaponry rules.

In some classrooms, these "Lego and Tinkertoy rules" are the subject of endless debates among staff and testing between children and teachers. I find the most common reason staff can't agree on these rules and stay consistent in their enforcement of them is that they don't really agree on whether pretend guns should be allowed in the classroom at all, and they haven't figured out how to talk about it. These unspoken staff conflicts result in confusion and limit testing among the children. Some teachers say no to almost everything and say they are doing it to keep children and materials safe, but they really would prefer to outlaw weapons altogether. They don't feel they can be straightforward about their opinions, because other staff may not share them. But what are we modeling for children when we do that?

While every rule can't be thought of in advance and written down, it's better for your staff to clarify your overall approach to weapons and superhero play before you get into the details of which building blocks can be used where. See chapter 7, "Working with Families and Staff," for further discussion.

Using Children's Healthy Impulses to Redirect Play

Whatever rules you choose to create for superhero play, remember that young children don't learn much from being told no. The first consequence teachers often use when a child breaks a rule is loss of privileges and sometimes physical punishment, but that rarely succeeds in changing the child's behavior. Unless the teacher is willing to look at alternative discipline methods, the punishments can become more and more severe without having any effect, except to flatten the child's self-esteem. Children have to be stopped when they are unsafe, but they learn more by being shown what they can do than by being punished. Redirection based on children's healthy impulses is one way teachers can respond positively to superhero play when it becomes unsafe.

Redirection is a time-honored practice in early childhood education. When children are doing something inappropriate, parents and teachers can guide them to an activity that is similar, but safe. If Superman is climbing the fences, set up a challenging climbing structure for him to conquer. If a monster is throwing blocks, give her a soft ball. If Aquaman is carrying water into the reading area, show him the water table. Superhero play offers a number of opportunities for effective redirection, as long as the technique is done with care.

Redirection works best when teachers pay attention to children's healthy impulses. These are the feelings, needs, desires, and goals that underlie and motivate unacceptable behavior. When young children misbehave, they often have a perfectly reasonable goal, but choose an ineffective strategy to get what they want. For example:

> *Malina, age four, and Stan, age three, are building a*
> *spaceship out of blocks as part of their robot explorer*
> *game. Benton, age three, wants to join the play, but he*

can't figure out how. He observes from ten feet away with a frown on his face. Suddenly, he rushes over, yells, "No!" and kicks the spaceship apart, then hides behind the couch. Malina and Stan are shocked. Malina yells, "We hate you!" Stan yells, "You can never play with us again!" Benton starts to cry.

Benton's objective is to play with friends, an admirable goal. However, like many preschoolers who are just beginning to experiment with social interactions, he doesn't know how to get what he wants. In fact, he probably assumes that Malina and Stan will refuse him, and he is already angry about it before he even approaches them.

If the teacher reacts by punishing Benton for his behavior, what will he learn? She may think she is teaching a lesson in safety and manners, but Benton's focus was on his desire for friendship. What he will hear is that his healthy impulse is wrong, and that the adults don't want him to have friends. That's not what he needs to hear! While Benton has to learn that he can't kick over other people's buildings, what he is really looking for is some guidance on better ways to approach his peers: "It looks like you want to play with them. Do you want some help figuring out what to do?" If an observant adult had approached him before he kicked the blocks and helped him put his feelings into words, the scenario might have had a more satisfying ending.

Young children often misinterpret punishment to mean that their underlying motivations are wrong, a problem that only leads to lower self-esteem and more misbehavior. Helping children fulfill their healthy impulses while setting clear limits on unacceptable strategies is a much more effective way to change behavior than punishing them or just telling them no. It gives the message that, while unsafe behaviors will be stopped, feelings, desires, and needs are always accepted. Redirection based on children's healthy impulses encourages self-awareness while modeling listening skills, empathy, and respect.

However, underlying needs and feelings can be difficult to gauge. There is no formula that guarantees success. The healthy impulse of one child who is throwing blocks may be that she wants to practice aiming and throwing, so giving her a ball and a target outside would work well. But another child may be throwing blocks to express anger, and the ball and target won't help. Redirecting her successfully would involve helping her express her feelings in words. And if she is throwing blocks to show she wants to play with another child but can't figure out how to do it, giving her a ball and moving her away is a distraction from her goal. She may need hints about how to ask a friend to play, just like Benton did when he destroyed his friends' building. Even the best teachers often get it wrong.

That's okay, because children don't need perfection. They appreciate adults who care enough to pay attention, and they can be very forgiving of wrong guesses. They need teachers who will ask about feelings, rather than tell children how they feel. Successful redirection requires sympathetic listening and dialogue, not an all-knowing authority figure. It's a guessing game that requires knowing children's histories, carefully observing their body language, maintaining sympathy for what they are trying to do, and believing that they are doing the best thinking they can. Assessing healthy impulses is an art, not a science.

Redirecting children is not the same as distracting them. *Distraction* is an attempt to get children to ignore their feelings and needs. Distraction can be useful when it allows children to step back from overwhelming emotions. Taking a break from a querulous Powerpuff chase game to read a book or listen to music can give the participants a chance to calm down and try again. However, adults tend to use distraction when they run out of patience, or when a child's feelings make them uncomfortable. Then it often involves bribing children with toys or food to make them happy. Redirection focuses on the child's feelings; distraction is about the adult's feelings. When teachers and parents constantly distract children, they are missing opportunities to help them learn better ways to handle their emotions.

What does redirecting superhero play look like? I find redirection most helpful when children are attempting physical challenges in the play that are too dangerous. Stopping or distracting them won't take away their desire to test the limits of their bodies. You will have more success keeping the play safe if you redirect it into activities that have clear safety rules, but still challenge their physical competence.

To create new physical challenges, watch the children to see what abilities they are working on—strength, speed, accuracy, coordination, or balance. Try to create substitutes that are exciting and demand similar skills. Watch out for activities that keep children interested through competition, though—they often end up being fun for only a few children. Here are some examples of redirected activities that have worked for teachers:

★ For high kickers

   Hang one or more plastic bottles from a tree branch or overhead beam. Place protective matting below. Start with the bottles low to the ground. Let the children take turns kicking the bottles. As the children learn to kick and fall safely, raise the bottles. Make sure you have lots of bottles around, and a place to recycle them!

★ For karate choppers

Use foam blocks, pieces of cardboard, or rolled-up newspaper pages as a substitute for boards, bricks, and necks.

★ For kung fu fighters

Try slowing down the action with superhero disco. Put on danceable music. Ask the children to show you how superheroes move, but in slow motion and without touching anyone else. As the children show they can dance safely, ask them to increase their speed, until they are dancing in fast motion. You can also stop the music periodically and ask the superheroes to freeze.

★ For high jumpers

For those who would like to fly off the top of the climbing structure, set up a place to jump that is between 2 and 4 feet high, using boards, blocks, hay bales, tables, or other equipment surrounded by mats. Hold a plastic hoop in various positions and heights and let children jump through, one at a time. As children become proficient, they can try doing tricks—jumping backward, turning in midair, rolling when they hit the mat, jumping in pairs, jumping through two hoops at once. Once children get used to the activity, they can help hold the hoops.

★ For high throwers

Tie hoops to a high branch. Throw balls, rolled-up papers, or sponges through the hoops.

★ For target shooters

Tape a large piece of paper (at least 4 feet long by 2½ feet wide) to a fence. Cover the surrounding area with plastic. Draw several circles or other targets on the paper. Give the children small foam balls or pieces of sponge and shallow containers of tempera paints. Let them dip the balls in paint and throw them at the targets as hard as they can. Younger children will need to be just a few feet away, while early-elementary children can be up to 10 feet away. Older children can try throwing the paint balls at the paper while running.

★ For high-wire artists

Create an obstacle course of boards to walk on and balance. Older children can try doing it while wearing a stack of hats or carrying balanced blocks.

★ For professional wrestling fans

Set up organized wrestling. Cover an area at least 6 by 6 feet with mats. Place chairs or carpet squares around the mats for spectators. Only two children can wrestle at a time, with an adult as referee. The safety rules must be clearly stated and strictly enforced:

- Pushing, grabbing, and squeezing are okay, but not around the neck or head.
- No hitting, kicking, scratching, or biting.
- If someone goes off the mat, start over.
- Either wrestler can say "Stop" at any time.
- Listen to the referee.

There doesn't have to be a winner or loser—the wrestlers continue until the referee decides to call the end of the round. You can use a bell to mark the rounds. I try to match up children of similar size until I learn each child's skill level. I'm always surprised when my smallest child takes my biggest superhero to the mat several times in a row!

★ For chasers and racers

Choose a path and set flags or other markers along it. Have children run the course as quickly as possible, touching all the markers. The path can include a climbing structure, a bar to jump over, or other obstacles.

★ For punchers

Set up a punching bag by stuffing a pillowcase with rags and hanging it on a short rope. Or send balloons or beach balls flying by punching them as hard as possible.

★ For musclemen and -women

Children want to test their strength, but giving them heavy objects to lift can be dangerous. Try using well-floured rolling pins to roll playdough out as thin as possible. Borrow large spring-clamps from a carpenter and let children squeeze them and clamp them onto wood (but not onto people). Tie a rope to a tire and let children take turns pulling it across the playground.

Redirection can also be used when children want to play together as a group, but are using negative strategies like exclusion or name-calling to bond with each other, or when there are battles for the group's leadership. Facilitating these disputes can be exhausting for everyone involved. Sometimes, children need a break from it, and can be quite relieved when adults temporarily take over the leadership role. Here are some organized activities that can foster group superhero cooperation:

★ Tire Pull

Instead of one child pulling a tire, attach several ropes to several tires that are tied together. Let teams of superheroes pull the tires across the playground, over an obstacle course, or up to the top of the climbing structure.

★ Blastoff, Part 1

Draw chalk "planets" in different colors around the yard. Tell children which color to look for, then count down to zero, and let all the Rocketeers blast off to the next planet. You can also use numbers, letters, or shapes for targets. If you want to emphasize group cooperation, children can hold onto a rope or plastic hoop and run together.

★ Blastoff, Part 2

Place several soft balls in the middle of a parachute or large sheet. Have children grab the edges. Count down to zero and send the balls high into the air. See how many come down in the parachute. Try it with stuffed animals or balloons.

★ Squirrels, Change Trees

Set up more chairs than children, and have everybody choose one. Play music or tell a squirrel story. Yell, "Squirrels, change trees." Everyone runs around and ends up in a different chair. Start again. If you don't have any squirrels in your class, try bears changing caves or spiders changing webs. It's musical chairs with no losers. A game only preschoolers could love!

★ Box City

Big boxes make great trains, rocket ships, caves, and other superhero homes and vehicles. Let the children draw doors and windows and have an adult cut them out with a knife. Decorate with paint and markers. Connect boxes with strapping tape to make shared structures. Add carpet squares, pillows, and blankets to make them cozy. Use chalk or masking tape to create roads between the buildings and bring in small trucks to make deliveries.

★ Animal Rescue Hide-and-Seek

Hide stuffed animals around the playground or classroom. When children find one, they should call for the animal rescue team. Groups of children can rush over with a blanket or cot "stretcher" and carry the animal to an animal hospital for care.

Helping Children Become More Aware of Safety Issues

Another way to reduce the amount of limit setting staff must do is to teach children how to spot potential danger. Many times, children don't know they are being unsafe until someone gets hurt or a teacher reprimands them. I find it helpful to use a system I call *safety check*. Safety checks provide a framework for intervening in superhero play without disrupting it. Here's an example:

> *Four children, ages four and five, are building a Batmobile out of cardboard boxes and blocks. They have stacked the materials at all angles, and one of the boxes is collapsing with a child inside.*
>
> *Teacher: Safety check! I want to make sure your car is safe.*
>
> *Shane, age four: It's safe! It's very strong and fast. We won't get hurt even if we crash.*
>
> *Teacher: But I'm looking at those blocks, and they look like they're about to fall over.*
>
> *Annie, age five: Yeah, they are. (She straightens them.)*
>
> *Teacher: Is it safe now?*
>
> *Annie: Yeah.*
>
> *Teacher: How can you tell?*
>
> *Annie: The top one was right by the edge. I put it right on top so it won't fall down.*
>
> *Teacher: Are there any other blocks that look unsafe?*
>
> *Orin, age five: There's another one over there. (He fixes it.)*
>
> *Teacher: Is there anything else that looks unsafe to you?*
>
> *Everyone: No!*
>
> *Teacher: There's another place that looks unsafe to me. I'm worried about Salvio in that box.*
>
> *Salvio, age four: Yeah, I'm getting smashed up.*

Sean: We better take the blocks off.

Teacher: Yes, and you can't climb up on the box either.

Annie: We're too heavy.

Salvio: You're too heavy!

Teacher: It looks like the safety check is over. Have fun with your car!

Orin: Safety check is over! Emergency! We have to save the hospital from getting blown up! Let's go!

Children learn that play has to stop during safety checks—not because adults are being mean, but because adults are trying to show them how to protect themselves. I do a safety check not only when I see something that might be dangerous, but when I see children playing safely as well. When I "catch them being safe," they're always very proud!

I start the year pointing out physical safety problems, then start bringing up social and emotional issues as well:

Three girls, age four, are playing Superwoman. They grab toys from other children, saying things like, "You're too weak. I'll do it, I'm Superwoman." Some children like it; others protest.

Teacher: Safety check!

Randy, age four: No, teacher, we're being safe, we're helping people but we're being very careful.

Teacher: I can see you're not hurting anyone's body, but I see you're hurting people's feelings. That's not safe.

Virginia, age five: You said I was stupid. That hurt my feelings!

Sarna, age four: But we're so strong 'cause we're Superwomen. We help people.

Teacher: How can you help people without hurting their feelings?

Virginia: Don't call names.

Teacher: What should they do?

Virginia: Ask kids if they want help. I don't want help.

Sarna: Does anybody want help? We're Superwomen.

Carla, age three: I do!

Teacher: Is there anything else unsafe that you can see?

Randy: No.

Teacher: Then the safety check is over.

Once children understand the safety check routine, they often use it without the teachers and look for safety problems on their own. By getting safety checks established early in the year, I can use it to redirect unsafe superhero play without making children feel bad about their game. Many children are able to step out of their fantasy roles, perform a safety check, and go back to their play, and they are more likely to stay safe because they were involved in figuring out what the problem was.

Negotiating with Children about Their Ideas

When teachers use their power fairly and respectfully to set and enforce limits, they are modeling exactly what they want children to learn in superhero play. Setting the classroom rules and keeping everyone safe is the teacher's responsibility, but when they are old enough, children deserve the chance to help set some of those rules. Involving children in this process teaches them that people feel respected when everyone feels empowered, rather than one group always deciding for another. As part of these dialogues, teachers can also find out more about what children are seeking in their play, provide explanations about why the adults have created particular rules, and bring up some adult concerns for children to consider. If children are to help set the rules, they have to be able to take into account the grown-ups' concerns, as well as their own.

Using guided conflict resolution techniques during children's daily disagreements sets the stage for these discussions. With help from adults, children can learn to put into words what they want, listen to other people, come up with creative solutions, compromise, and select an action everyone agrees on. The more experience children have with conflict resolution, the more they will be able to understand other people's points of view, an important skill for them to have before they can help set rules that are fair for everyone. For more about helping children solve their own disputes, see the section on developing children's sense of justice in chapter 6, "Fostering Heroism."

A discussion with young children about limits is not the same as a conversation. When teachers talk informally with young children, they usually use active listening techniques to follow the children's lead. They ask questions that help the children turn their thoughts into words, then repeat the words so the children can judge whether they have said what they wanted to say. The adult does lots of listening, and lets the conversation wander. In a guided dialogue about rules, the teacher still uses her listening skills, but she also asks questions that keep it on track, and brings in more of the adult perspective.

Here's a set of rules generated by a group of three- and four-year-olds about how to handle some visiting baby chickens. They were playing and studying birds, and a family brought them in for a morning:

Rules for the Chickies

No chasing them, scaring them, or hitting them.
Don't put them in baby clothes.
Don't put them on not balanced stuff.
Don't put them on top of each other.
Feed them the right stuff.
Don't ever make the chickies sneeze.
Don't put them in your shoes.
Don't hold them by their fingernails.
Don't forget where you put them.
Don't throw them or juggle them in the air.

Expressing adult ideas in ways that young children can understand is a difficult skill, one that requires thought, practice, and patience. Preschoolers are not ready to hear all our concerns about violence, racism, and sexism, and how they impact superhero play. They don't share our knowledge of social history, or our worries about the future. They can only grasp what applies to the smaller world they are studying, the world of family, friends, school, and community. The teacher's job is to simplify adult ideas and show how they apply to that world.

Rules about gun play are particularly difficult for many adults to negotiate. The feelings people carry about them are passionate and complex. Many teachers are appalled by the sight of children pretending to shoot each other, and their sense of urgency and pain makes it hard to listen to children's ideas about them without preaching.

The following is a dialogue between Carmen, a teacher, and Marti, age two and a half. I was observing, and wrote it down as it happened. Note that the teacher makes her best guess at what the child wants, because he is too young to express it himself. She gives a few choices while setting clear limits, and she briefly brings in an adult point of view without expecting Marti to respond to it. She tries to come up with a solution that is acceptable to Marti and engages his creativity. When other children get involved, she sets up a game that involves them in large motor activity:

Marti: (Pointing a long block at the teacher) Shoot! Shooter! Shoot!

Carmen: You like to make that noise.

Marti: Shooter! Shooter! Shoot!

Carmen: Do you want to play a shooting game?

Marti: Shoot!

Carmen: You can play that game with your fingers, outside. The block isn't safe for a shooting game.

Marti: Shoot! Shoot!

Carmen: I don't want to play a shooting game. I'll show you where you can play that game. (She takes Marti's hand and leads him to the door.) I want you to leave the block inside. (She sets the block aside.) Do you want to shoot at the hay bale or at a paper on the fence?

Marti: Shoot! Shoot! (Points his finger at the teacher.)

Carmen: (Kneeling down) Are you mad at me because I took the block away?

Marti: I'm mad.

Carmen: I'll show you where you can shoot.

Marti: Shoot! Shoot!

Carmen: I don't want you to shoot at me. That makes me think about real guns. Real guns hurt people, and I don't like that. If you want to play with pretend guns, you can shoot paper.

Marti: No! I want the block.

Carmen: Did that block make you feel big and strong?

Marti: Yeah. Shoot! Shoot!

Carmen: Now you're shooting with your whole arm. That's a new idea. Does that help you feel big and strong?

Marti: Yeah.

Carmen: I could tape the paper on your arm like this. (Wraps the paper around her own arm.)

Marti: Yeah! Yeah!

Carmen: Do you want to color the paper first?

Marti: Yeah.

Carmen: Let's go get you some crayons.

(She brings out crayons. Marti colors, and then wants the picture taped around his arm. Other children join, and want to wrap various parts of their bodies.)

Marti: Shoot! Shoot!

Carmen: Olma, do you want Marti to shoot you?

Olma: No!

Carmen: Olma says, "No." I'll put up lots of places to shoot on the fence. You'll have to run hard to find them all.

(She puts up three pieces of paper in a portion of the yard, away from another group playing in the sand. Several children, including Marti, run from one paper to the other, shooting at them.)

The next dialogue was one I had with Ray, age four and a half; Enjay, age four; Melinda, age five; and Shawn, age four. My aide and I reconstructed this dialogue afterward, so it isn't complete. These older children are much more capable of making group decisions, talking about media influences, and recognizing adult viewpoints.

They come up with a game that works for the group, for other children, and for the teacher.

> *The children are wearing sections of glitter-covered cardboard tubes on their upper arms. They have long weapons made from pieces of rolled-up newspaper and are waving them as they run around doing martial arts kicks, confronting other children. Enjay, the group leader, wears his sweater tied around his neck as a cape.*
>
> *Teacher: Enjay, I'm hearing a lot of people saying no to this game. What are you playing?*
>
> *Enjay: Power Rangers! I'm the blue.*
>
> *Melinda: I'm a red Power Ranger.*
>
> *Teacher: What do Power Rangers do in this game?*
>
> *Enjay: They fight.*
>
> *Melinda: They kill bad monsters.*
>
> *Ray: I'm a robot Power Ranger.*
>
> *Teacher: It looks like those armbands make you feel very powerful.*
>
> *Enjay: These are power tubes. They give us so much power that we can kill any monsters.*
>
> *Teacher: Is that what Power Rangers do on the TV show?*
>
> *Enjay: Power Rangers are in the movies. They fight the monsters and they turn into robots with colors and guns and things.*
>
> *Teacher: So people turn into Power Rangers and fight monsters.*
>
> *Everyone: Yeah!*
>
> *Teacher: Why are they fighting the monsters?*

Ray: Monsters are very bad, so they have to be blown up. They're very scary and bad.

Teacher: Are they real? Are they really in the world where you can see them?

Everyone: Yes!

Enjay: And we have to kill them.

Teacher: I'm not seeing any real monsters at our school. Are you pretending other children are the monsters?

Enjay: Yeah, then we kill them.

Teacher: But everyone is saying no to you. That must be frustrating.

Ray: Yeah, we hate them.

Teacher: You don't like it when people say no. Rachel (age four, who has been listening on the side), do you want to be a monster in their game?

Rachel: No! That's too scary.

Shawn: Pow! Pow!

Rachel: No! You're so stupid.

Teacher: (Stepping between Shawn and Rachel) Shawn, you don't have Rachel's permission to shoot her. If you can't stop, I'll have you put your costume away. Do you still want to play?

Shawn: Yes.

Teacher: Here's the problem. You want to be Power Rangers, but nobody else wants to be monsters. What do you think we should do?

Ray: We can shoot the people over the fence.

Teacher: A lot of people don't like shooting guns, even pretend ones.

Ray: My mom and dad hate guns.

Teacher: Why do you think they hate guns?

Ray: Too many people get hurt.

Enjay: These are just pretend guns. We don't use real guns.

Shawn: My mom hates guns, but I like them.

Teacher: Can you play guns at your house?

Shawn: I can shoot the lights and things. It's just pretend.

Teacher: What do you like about pretend guns?

Shawn: I don't know.

Teacher: It looks like you feel very powerful when you use them.

Enjay: Yeah, like Power Rangers!

Melinda: We have lots of power!

Teacher: Well, what should we do? You can only use pretend guns.

Everyone: No! No real guns!

Ray: Somebody could die for real.

Teacher: So you want to use pretend guns for a power shooting game.

Everyone: Yeah!

Teacher: How can you do it safely?

Melinda: We could shoot the clouds and the sky.

Ray and Shawn: No.

Enjay: We could make a monster.

Others: Yeah, we could make one.

Teacher: What could you use?

Melinda: I'm gonna draw a big monster called Gally Gally.

Ray: Mine is Bad Guy.

Shawn: Mine is Bad Guy Pony, right?

Enjay: We could make a monster box. We could glue our monsters on the box. But we can't kick it, or we'll break it.

Melinda: We could kick, but not for real, for pretend.

Others: Yeah.

Teacher: That sounds safe. I'll let you do that, because the monster isn't a real person.

Knowing When to Stop Superhero Play

There are times when superhero play can become inappropriate or dangerous, despite all attempts by the teaching staff to enforce rules respectfully and turn the play into a positive experience. As part of their fantasies, children can forget that their bodies aren't designed for flying off high places or breaking bricks with their hands. They may not remember that their light sabers and blaster bullets are really wooden blocks that hurt when they make contact. They can get so involved in fighting bad guys that they attack other children with both fists and words. They can continue to use harmful racial, ethnic, and gender slurs. Even if these players calm down and agree to be safe, the minute they slip back into their fantasy roles the agreements can be forgotten.

If the danger is too great or if it keeps recurring, then the teacher has to take charge. Even the most experienced and sympathetic teacher may not be able to ensure the safety of all the children under her care when her superheroes get too wrapped up in their quest for power. That's when further restrictions and temporary bans on superhero play may be needed.

An important question to ask when thinking about stopping superhero play is, "Am I seeing any immediate physical or emotional danger?" If there is, then interrupt the play. If the game continues to be unsafe despite your efforts, it's time to put a halt to superhero play, at least temporarily. But if there is no immediate danger, then take a deep breath. Ask yourself what part of the play is setting off your alarms. You may still decide to intervene, but you can take some time to plan your response, and the children and families may be able to help.

That doesn't mean you have to wait for superheroes to hurt each other before taking action. Intervention is always more successful when done before misbehavior or danger happens. Experienced teachers rely on children's voices, words, facial expressions, body language, and history to tell them when a situation is about to explode. They can often tell when two teams or personalities are about to collide, or when a play fight is becoming serious. They can hear when the joyous laughter in a chase game turns to anger and fear. They also know that some children who would normally be able to control their impulses and pay attention to the needs of others can lose those skills in the middle of an exciting superhero game. By using careful observation and educated intuition, you can judge when to interrupt the play. The goal of intervening early is to give players a chance to get what they want without having to stop the play completely.

A few children become so obsessed with superhero play, though, and so fixated on the scary images in their minds, that they can't stop hurting themselves or others. They play out the same scenes over and over, and can't leave their character behind even during meals, nap, and circle times. If those children are charismatic enough to become the classroom play leaders, their angry attitude can spread and become the norm. That's not an atmosphere that builds a sense of community! When I have not been able to counteract these situations quickly, I have stopped superhero play.

Some of these obsessed children will resist any attempt to alter their game, because they have fantasies and fears that they can't set aside. They may be dealing with difficult or impossible situations: being teased or abused by adults, siblings, or neighbors; watching inappropriate movies and TV shows without knowing how to filter out the scary images; witnessing violence in their homes or neighborhoods; being told that any display of fear is a sign of weakness. They may have concerns about losing friendships and social status, or they may be worried about going to kindergarten, having a new sibling, or experiencing some other big life change.

Stopping the play of obsessed children and banning their weapons may help a teacher regain control of the classroom, but it can leave the children feeling angry and isolated. These children still need a way to work out their feelings and stay attached to the classroom community. Other curriculum activities should focus on making sure they are reintegrated. Storytelling can allow them to express their fears safely. Structured group games can help them rebuild their friendships and keep their place in the social fabric of the group. Classroom "helper" jobs can help them feel powerful and mend their relationships with adults.

Working with families to eliminate stressful situations at home is also essential, but there is no guarantee of success. Some families are open to change, but are unaware that the TV and movies they watch or the ways they talk about feelings can have a strong impact on their children's play. Some are aware that their behavior affects their children, but they need help finding alternatives. Others will not talk about their home lives at all, and see any questions as intrusions or accusations. As teachers, we don't have the power to eliminate many of the damaging influences we see in our students' lives. Working with families on these underlying issues can be difficult and frustrating, but when home and school do cooperate, the need for discipline and rules can be greatly reduced.

In my experience, once these obsessed superheroes are convinced that their needs will not be ignored, many of them are relieved to have an adult take charge. One five-year-old even commented, "This is better. I wish we had stopped before." They don't like feeling out of control, but they don't know what else to do. Some of these seemingly powerful children will then choose a very different kind of play when their superhero routines are stopped, such as baby play, complete with bottles, diapers, and cribs.

When teachers have to stop or restrict superhero play, and they do it thoughtfully, most of the children in the classroom recognize why it was done and move on to other activities. They are very aware that the classroom wasn't feeling safe, and they usually appreciate the change.

STORIES FROM THE CLASSROOM

Bad Guy Dolls

One of the ways I let children practice the skill of making classroom rules is by letting them create rules for dolls. The dolls in my classroom are not anonymous; they are members of the classroom community, with names and histories created by staff and children over several years. They participate in circle. They get real ice and bandages for their pretend accidents. When we make murals of all the hands in the class, we help the dolls add their handprints. When we make charts about our skin or hair or eye colors, they are included. When the children make up stories during their play, the dolls are often the main characters. And when the dolls play, they have to follow the rules.

The dolls are located throughout the classroom, not just in the housekeeping corner. That way, the children get to discuss the limits in all learning areas of the school. The doll named Jalen hangs out in the art area. Jalen's story is that he is three years old, lives with his father and grandmother, and likes to dress all in green. When children are busy with an art project, I put him in the middle of the table where he can listen to them talk about their creations. The doll named Rosie prefers the outdoors, while her older brother, Marco, tends to stay in the book area so children can read to him.

Eileen is a doll who is four and has two moms and a pet rabbit. She likes to build with blocks and play make-believe. She sits on the shelf in the block area, where children construct a hospital for her when she is playing doctor, an airplane when she is a pilot, or a barn when she is wearing her horse costume. When children are playing superhero games, she wants the same clothes and power accessories as the children. She shoots other dolls with her pretend gun, and gets into arguments with them.

We don't allow children to mistreat the dolls, any more than we allow children to hurt each other. So when my children set up a cardboard box in the block area and started throwing dolls in jail for a variety of pretend crimes (sometimes from a great distance), some staff members were concerned. They weren't sure we should allow the play to continue. Several teachers thought we should ban the game because the dolls might get

damaged. One tried to redirect the throwing into a bean bag toss game, but no one was interested. Others were more concerned about labeling the dolls as bad when we had worked hard to make them members of the community. They were particularly worried because several of the dolls that were members of racial and ethnic minorities seemed to be targeted for this treatment. I agreed to bring up the issue with the children at group time.

We brought all the dolls to circle the next day, and I asked them how they felt about the "bad guy doll" game. They each got a turn to speak. (Of course, I do the talking for them, but no one seems to mind.) Marco and Eileen said they liked the game. Rosie said she wouldn't mind it if we played it outside, but Jalen didn't like the game at all. Marco was a little worried that people would think he really was a bad guy, but the children said they knew it was just pretend. Eileen wanted to make sure she got to be a police officer sometimes, so everyone decided to take turns.

The children agreed to come up with some rules for the game that took the dolls' opinions into account, and I wrote them down:

- No spanking the prisoners.
- No hitting the prisoners.
- No kicking the prisoners.
- If prisoners are hungry, give them food.
- If prisoners have to poop or pee, they shouldn't do it in the jail.
- Prisoners can get out of jail if they apologize or do something nice.
- Masking tape can be used on the prisoners' hands and feet, but not on their hair, and not on their mouths because then they can't talk.
- No throwing the prisoners unless they like it.
- All prisoners get out of jail at circle and lunch.
- Prisoners can sleep in jail at naptime if they want to.
- If a prisoner doesn't want to play, he can do something else.
- If a prisoner wants to be a police officer, give her a turn.
- The prisoners aren't really bad because they are just pretending.

"That's an excellent list," I said. "Does anybody have anything to add?"

One of the youngest in the classroom tentatively raised a hand. "Teacher," he said, "what's a prisoner?"

"It's a bad guy doll," said a four-year-old, and everyone agreed.

What did the children learn from this exercise? To take someone else's point of view, to think about how their actions have an impact on others, to compromise, and to work together as a group. I was able to refer to these rules later on, when children started throwing each other in jail. The list didn't solve every problem, but it made it much easier to start a conversation about keeping superhero play safe.

CHAPTER 4

Supporting Superhero Play

"I'm a firefighter ambulance driver. I drive the ambulance and help the dead people get all better, and I can put out the fire at the same time. That's why I have to hold two different hats."

—Leila, age three and a half, in October

"If you want to be a cat, you have to have these black ears that point up. They can be brown or white, too, but they have to point up. And a tail like this one, a long tail. And cat teeth. I can just pretend I have teeth. And claws. I need claws. Do we have any claws?"

—Leila, age four, in February

"Growl! I'm the fire monster! That's why everything is red. My dress is red, my hat is red, even my necklace. This is a fire necklace that shoots fire and kills other monsters. I kill everything, even the teachers, even the good guys. The best good guys in the world, even they have to die."

—Leila, age four, in April

WHILE SOME CHILDREN jump right into imaginary superhero roles as toddlers, most, like Leila, show an interest in other, more realistic dramatic play first. By observing and supporting this earlier play, teachers can establish expectations for appropriate behavior, observe group dynamics, and help children develop successful relationships and leadership styles. That makes it much easier to facilitate superhero play when it appears.

Planning for dramatic play means thinking about all the ingredients of your classroom: the physical environment, the curriculum, the children, the families, and the staff. Teachers can support superhero play by

- ★ Understanding how superhero play develops
- ★ Creating a classroom that welcomes play
- ★ Including children's ideas in the curriculum planning process
- ★ Encouraging transitional dramatic play
- ★ Providing props and play spaces that inspire superhero play

Understanding How Superhero Play Develops

When children begin dramatic play they usually don't start right out as superheroes. Superhero play typically develops through three broad stages. Children's earliest dramatic play is usually imitative, mirroring what they have seen in their families, out in their communities, and on TV. As Georgina, age three, said, "My dad is half dad and half doctor, and when I grow up I'm going to be half music teacher and half train engineer." Cooking, putting babies to sleep, and driving cars are some of the common beginning themes. In some classrooms, the dramatic play area is set up with dolls, dress-up clothes, and housekeeping equipment to encourage this play, but the equipment rarely changes.

As children get older and become more aware of the wider community, and as their imaginations expand, these realistic themes start to encompass more powerful or heroic roles, such as firefighter, police officer, truck driver, soldier, doctor, or construction worker. Teachers often set up props for this play outdoors because it involves more action. The play is still reality based, but it shows more fantasy and grandiose ideas. Here's an example:

> *Shane, age three: Pretend I'm a grown-up and I'm forty-four and my name is Petey.*
>
> *Mark, age four: And I'm a grown-up, too, right? And I'm building a road.*
>
> *Don, age three: Pretend this is my big shovel and we dig the hole with it.*
>
> *Shane: Mine really is a big shovel, and we have to be careful 'cause it's pointy.*
>
> *Mark: We need to dig from here all the way around the corner, right?*
>
> *Don: We can make a hole to put poison soup in.*

Some children jump directly from this reality-based play to fantasy-oriented superhero play. But there is often another, transitional stage that can provide rich dramatic play themes while giving teachers lots of opportunities to teach children how to play out fantasies safely. It includes roles and scenarios that have a fantasy or mythic component but still have a realistic basis. Kings and queens, knights and castles, pirates and treasure, volcanoes, and a wide array of animal characters live in this world. The themes of power and friendship so common to superhero play are all there, but with much less interference from commercial images, and the conflicts that arise are often solved without resorting to megaweapons and uncontrolled superpowers. I have found this transitional stage so satisfying for children and important to the success of later superhero play that I make a point of nurturing it every year.

Children make the jump into superhero play for a variety of reasons. Some have reached the point in their brain development where they can fully experience their imaginations. Sometimes this is joyful, and sometimes it's scary. Either way, the fantasies are compelling, and must be played out. Other children are following the play of peers or older children. They may not be able to fully imagine superhero fantasies, but they enjoy it because it is a "big kid" game or because it connects them in exciting ways to friends. Some get involved because of traumas in their lives—injuries, divorces, moves, or anything else that makes them feel less powerful. Others imitate characters and plots from new movies or TV shows or mimic disturbing images they have seen on the news. Smart teachers keep their ears open for shows that are heavily advertised or current events that will have an impact on children. They know that many of these images are not really appropriate for preschoolers, but that many preschoolers will get to watch them anyway, and that they are likely to show up in their classrooms. They can then think through how they will respond to these characters before they even appear.

The stages that lead up to fantasy-based superhero play are not always distinct. When children move from one stage of dramatic play to the next, it doesn't mean they completely abandon the earlier play. Plenty of superhero fans will still take a turn at being a knight or a doctor. But I have found understanding the sequence of realistic to transitional to superhero play useful when I am setting up my long-term curriculum goals and getting ready for superhero play.

Creating a Classroom that Welcomes Play

Is your classroom ready for dramatic play? A well-planned physical environment, especially outdoors, is important to welcoming the play. Many teachers in early childhood education spend a lot of time on their room arrangements, regularly changing the materials in the different play areas. They realize that young children learn best through hands-on, concrete experiences, rather than lectures and abstract lessons, so they frequently add new sensory and manipulative materials to support their curriculum ideas. Teachers have to pay attention to three different aspects of the classroom environment when they are creating curriculum: the built-in equipment, the adult-moveable equipment, and the child-moveable materials. The way they arrange these elements can determine whether their learning plans, including those for superhero play, will succeed.

The built-in elements of a classroom and playground are the things that cannot be changed easily, such as the walls, cabinets, decks, sandboxes, and climbing structures. These help determine what activities teachers can plan in any area. Is the sandbox big enough for the dragon cave the children want to build, or would it work better under the climber? Is there a sidewalk that wagons can drive on so superheroes can transport rescued people to a play hospital? Is there a quiet space where two or three children can build a miniature block castle? Can a spaceport be set up outdoors on the grass or indoors in the block area, or both? Sometimes a school is designed for play, and the built-in elements make the job easier; sometimes teachers have to work hard to compensate for a badly conceived classroom. Teachers gradually learn which activities and dramatic play themes work in different parts of their classrooms.

The second layer of the environment is the adult-movable equipment. Teachers change the classroom by moving furniture, carpets, shelves, mats, and other large equipment. They also add pictures, bulletin boards, and other decorations. These materials allow staff to define play areas, control traffic patterns, and give children clues about curriculum themes. Teaching in a classroom where nothing can be moved or posted on the walls is frustrating!

The third layer is the child-movable equipment—the toys, sand, water, art materials, puzzles, dress ups, dolls, and small furniture that help children express themselves and feel in control of their environment. In dramatic play areas, these materials can help children decide what games to play and roles to take, such as grocery clerk, cook, puppy, mechanic, or astronaut. Some schools have theme kits that store a variety of props related to one kind of play in one box. Experienced teachers regularly look for new ways to support dramatic play themes using the materials they have on hand. Children are always ready to use those materials in new and surprising ways to play out their fantasies.

Teachers often focus their attention on the child-movable materials when they are planning curriculum, but all three layers are important. Each gives children clues to what can happen in a play area. If a well-defined dramatic play area has pictures of doctors and nurses on the walls; cots and blankets; a shelf with white shirts, bandages, and a bag of medical tools; and several books about the hospital, then children are more likely to play a hospital game without destroying the materials.

The areas teachers set up with these three layers of equipment are called learning centers. A typical classroom has a variety of learning centers geared to particular activities, such as an art area, block area, dramatic play corner, and reading area. Some areas may serve more than one purpose—the block area may be the place where circle time is held, and the art tables may get used for lunch. Learning centers let children know where they can find space and materials for their ideas and help adults think about their curriculum plans. If a teacher wants to set up painting indoors, she usually does it in the art area. If children want to set up a rocket ship in the middle of that activity, the teacher usually directs them to a more appropriate part of the room, where the play is less likely to interrupt others. In a well-designed classroom, there is a lot of room for flexibility, but everything doesn't happen everywhere.

Many teachers forget that the outdoor space, where superhero games often take place, is also part of the classroom, and can be set up with learning centers in mind.

Outdoor learning centers are a little different from indoor centers. Instead of spaces set aside for particular activities, like art and block play, a playground can be divided into activity zones for high-, medium-, and low-active play. Highly active play, which engages children's whole bodies as they move through space, includes climbing structures, tire swings, bike paths, and open grass. Moderately active play, which also centers on large motor activities but does not involve a lot of moving through the yard, can happen in sandboxes, on decks, in sensory tables, and in playhouses. Less active play, such as reading, artwork, puzzles, and resting, requires tables or small, protected soft areas (although some children choose swings as a place to be alone and relax). The borders of activity zones are marked by fences, shelves, sand barriers, benches, and changes in ground cover. These, along with climbing structures, are usually built-in elements of the playground.

In many schools, teachers add child-moveable materials like sand toys, bikes, and balls to these built-in elements and don't do any other planning for outdoor play. But the layer that is missing, the teacher-moveable equipment, is crucial to the success of play. Outdoor learning centers usually have to be more flexible than indoor centers. A grass area may be used for a highly active chase game, a moderately active pretend picnic, or a less active painting project. The climbing structure may be the scene of a busy pirate ship or a quieter house game. Teachers can use a combination of teacher- and child-moveable materials to make these changes clear to children. Blankets, traffic cones, portable dividers, cardboard boxes, and tables are all useful ways to give children clues about how to use a space. Musical instruments on a deck will have a much better chance of coexisting with the Ninja Turtles on the climbing structure next to it if you put the instruments on large blankets and protect them with a few room dividers or chairs.

When the outdoor space is designed with activity zones and learning centers in mind, superhero and other highly active play can coexist with other interests. Books, art materials, and other quiet materials will be safe to use outdoors. On playgrounds where there is no clear delineation of outdoor spaces, children get the message that everything can happen everywhere. The loudest, most active games tend to wipe out the quieter games. Superhero play destroys every other game in the yard, until everyone in the class has either joined the pack or is hiding behind the teacher's leg. I encourage teachers to figure out what they have available to divide their yard into activity zones, and to introduce children to the expectation that quieter curriculum activities will be protected. At first, children will need to be reminded about the borders, but once children get used to the idea they will start to request them to protect their own play. If teachers do this well before superhero play appears, activity zones will be easier to maintain when children start to use bad guy roles as an excuse to break the rules.

For more information on curriculum planning, learning centers, and materials for dramatic play, try these books:

Barbour, Ann, and Blanche Desjean-Perrotta. *Prop Box Play: Fifty Themes to Inspire Dramatic Play.* Beltsville, MD: Gryphon House, 2002.

Brokering, Lois. *Resources for Dramatic Play.* Columbus, OH: McGraw-Hill, 1990.

Curtis, Deb, and Margie Carter. *Reflecting Children's Lives: A Handbook for Planning Child-Centered Curriculum.* St. Paul: Redleaf Press, 1996.

Curtis, Deb, and Margie Carter. *Designs for Living and Learning.* St. Paul: Redleaf Press, 2003.

Diffily, Deborah, Elizabeth Donaldson, and Charlotte Sassman. *The Scholastic Book of Early Childhood Learning Centers.* New York: Scholastic Professional Press, 2001.

Kohl, Maryann F. *Making Make-Believe: Fun Props, Costumes, and Creative Play Ideas.* Beltsville, MD: Gryphon House, 2002.

Including Children's Ideas in the Curriculum Planning Process

Two other elements of the classroom are important to consider when getting ready for superhero play. One of them, a set of clear and fair rules, was discussed in the previous chapter. The other is a curriculum planning process that includes ideas for play gathered from the children, families, and staff.

There is no single, correct way to plan curriculum for young children. However, teachers will have a hard time supporting superhero play if their activities are all based on long-term plans that pay no attention to children's lives and interests. The best curriculum takes at least some of its cues from the children, and uses the ideas that emerge to teach the academic and other skills they need as they get older.

Observation can help teachers discover the play themes that will hold children's attentions. Do they like cooking with sand outdoors? Would they rather diaper babies and put them to sleep? Are they fascinated by changes in the weather? Do they want to learn more about machines? Are they talking about a particular movie, TV program, or toy, and is there a way to tap into their attraction without turning the classroom into a media advertisement? Is there a theme that engages a group of children, or are there many separate interests? What do the play leaders want? What about the children who need some special attention? What materials and activities do the staff have to support the play they see? Plans that teachers develop from the children's interests are called *emergent curriculum,* and they help children feel they have some ownership and control of the classroom.

Keeping in touch with children's families can also give teachers good ideas for play, because parents can tell you what is going on in their homes and neighborhoods, and what interests and experiences their children have outside of school. If several families have new babies, a pretend diapering area might work well. If some of the children have been watching an old building being torn down in the neighborhood, the staff could create a safe place for young construction workers to demolish block structures or cardboard boxes. An older brother or sister who is involved in a sport or hobby may be willing to come in and give a demonstration that will spark new play.

Maintaining connections with families can also help teachers avoid misguided assumptions about what play should look like. For example, if the curriculum is about transportation and the staff wants to set up a place where children can pretend to drive to school, they can't assume everyone comes by car. Do some take the bus? The subway? A bicycle? A pickup truck? How can the dramatic play center reflect all of these options? If teachers are setting up a play kitchen, what kinds of equipment can they include that will reflect the backgrounds of all the children in their class? A canning pot? A tortilla press? A waffle iron? A rice steamer? A microwave? Parents will often lend materials that will make the play more familiar to their children and help teachers point out the similarities and differences among families.

Staff interests are also a consideration. Teachers often have particular themes that they enjoy exploring. One may have lots of information and activities about trains, and want to set up an outdoor train station when she sees children who are interested in transportation. Another may like talking about animal care, so she could create a veterinarian's office and gather information from families about the children's pets. Individual staff members may also have particular skills that they like to use to support play, so that one teacher may contribute songs and books to a curriculum theme, another might set up a puppet theater, and another might help children create their own play props at the carpentry bench. There's no reason curriculum can't be fun for teachers too! When adults enjoy what they are doing and share what they love, children are more likely to sustain interest.

Teachers can also extend the curriculum by occasionally joining in. Adults have to be careful not to take over children's play by becoming the leader and source of all ideas, but they can still participate by asking questions, giving suggestions, and even joining the play for brief periods to bring groups of children together and model safe behavior. The goal should be for the children to take as much control as possible, rather than providing a fun diversion for the adults.

Encouraging Transitional Dramatic Play

If you want to set the groundwork for safe superhero play, then spend time supporting earlier dramatic play, especially play that is transitional. To get children started on dramatic play that has more of a fantasy component, treasure hunting is always a great way to begin. Gold- and silver-painted rocks, wood, and walnuts; large colored beads; fake jewels; or shells can be buried in a sensory table or sandbox, tied into bushes, or hidden under furniture. Children can also hide them from adults. Older children enjoy making treasure maps and cardboard treasure boxes. The children can dig, sift, or use magnets, nets, or tongs to capture the treasure. Treasure hunting works well with a variety of dramatic play themes—pirates, castles, elves and fairies, and even field mice.

For groups that really enjoy digging, try burying treasures in the ground (up to a foot deep). Let the children dig them out, then bury more at the bottom of the hole they made. Over a period of six weeks, I had a group of four- and five-year-olds dig a hole 6 feet in diameter and 3 feet deep. We could have gone further, but we hit the automatic sprinkler lines—oops!

Powerful natural phenomena, like rain, wind, thunder, lightning, fire, volcanoes, and waves, are also very attractive to children during this transition stage and can stimulate a lot of play. There are many science and dramatic play experiments children can try as a group, such as the following:

★ Set up a wind zone by hanging strips of crepe paper, cloth, or yarn.

   Tie different-sized weights to the bottom of some of the strips. Ask children to create enough wind to move the strips using their breath, pieces of cardboard, and a variety of other materials. Show the children how to fan each other without touching. Blow bubbles, and use the fans to keep them up in the air. Pretend to be trees, flowers, feathers, or dandelion seeds in a gentle wind, then in a storm. Put out gym mats so your feathers and dandelion seeds can do somersaults and other tricks.

★ Pretend to be a rainstorm.

   Have the children pound on the floor with their feet or hands or sticks, getting louder and louder (but watch out for dusty rugs!). Give them pieces of paper or thin cardboard to shake for thunder. Flashlights always seem like a poor stand-in for lightning, but children love them.

★ Create a real rainstorm.

   Give children watering cans and let them pour water off the highest point in your playground, or off a second-floor balcony. Pour the water onto a variety of materials—plastic sheets, cloth, metal cookie sheets, dirt, cardboard—to see what makes the most convincing rain sound.

★ On a hot day, hang a hose from a high point and let the children play under it.

Adjust the nozzle so it sprays hard enough to be exciting, but not so hard that it stings. Give the children plastic bottles or big cans that will make noise under the spray. Give a group of children a sheet of clear plastic to put over their heads.

★ Use long pieces of cloth, a sheet, or a parachute to make waves.

Put small balls on the cloth to add to the action. It's hard for the youngest children to coordinate their wave movements, but older fours and up can usually work together to make the biggest waves possible. Ask children to make waves in their arms, legs, and whole bodies. Wave play fits in well with sea-life curriculum. Caution: tidal waves are a recurring nightmare for many children. They are big, powerful, impersonal, and destructive. Keep an eye out for children who are afraid of or obsessed with wave play.

★ Rivers and lakes are fun to make in sand and dirt areas.

Children love to dig water channels and create dams and waves while they learn about the physics of liquids and mud. Rocks, leaves, sticks, boats, and funnels add to the possibilities for learning. A hose left on "low" can feed the system, or children can fill it up with buckets. Be sure to find out from parents how comfortable they are with dirty, wet messes.

★ Don't forget volcanoes! Hot lava is a common image in children's play.

Create volcanoes by forming small mountains of sand or clay around plastic pipes or cups. Put in a tablespoon or more of baking soda, add a similar amount of vinegar, and watch your volcanoes foam. Adding red food color makes the lava look more realistic. Pretending to be dormant volcanoes that awaken and erupt is always a circle-time hit. I have a small collection of volcanic rocks that I display at my science table whenever play turns volcanic.

The dramatic play roles children choose during transitional play are often based on real people who have taken on the mythical status of kings and queens, princes and princesses, knights, and pirates. The availability of books and other materials with real pictures and information about these characters and their historical eras allows teachers to keep this play going for a long time. In my classroom one year, one child's interest in knights and sword fighting became the center of play for a group of ten three- and four-year-olds that lasted for three months. As part of the play, we allowed slow-motion sword fighting with foam tubes in one small area of the playground. We discussed their swords' magic powers:

Ariel: Mine squirts magic and mosquitoes.

Billy: Mine can throw fireballs.

Darrel: Mine can throw dragons all over the universe and land in the puddle of mud and fireballs, and put poison juice all over the mosquitoes and it goes in their eyes and they die.

Ron: My sword can transform and shoot fireballs.

Ariel: Mine can turn bad guys into frogs.

Sonya: Mine tapes the dragon's mouth and eyes, so she can't see or hear.

Billy: Mine could save a bat.

We created costumes and turned our outdoor climbing structure into a castle, called Golden Castle, by attaching large pieces of painted cardboard. Golden Castle had a sheet that the children painted for a roof, pulleys and buckets for hauling materials up and down, and a system of plastic pipes for communicating between levels. The children dug a moat in the sand, filled it with water, and used boards to create a drawbridge. We looked at books about castles for new ideas, and set out boxes, wood pieces, and glue to make small castles for tabletop fantasy play. Several of the children turned their obsession with dinosaurs into an interest in dragons, which became the castle guards. Watching a monarch butterfly emerge inspired a butterfly character, Boo Boo Bitsu, who needed rescuing from a monster, while another child's interest in Disney cartoons provided the magic words they used to battle monsters: *bibbity bobbity boo* (always shouted with first one, then the other, then both hands in the air). There was much debate among the players about whether to eliminate the monster with swords or with magic; magic won out.

As part of the Golden Castle play, I helped the children create a picture book. The process took about six weeks, with parts of the story written at circle time and parts during the play itself. Illustrations came from a wide variety of art projects, including three-dimensional paper swords, a butterfly on a paper plate, and a collage monster. I supported the writing at circle time by using two flannelboard characters, Juan and Marisol, and a castle made from gold foil. Readers who are familiar with my children's book, *Heroines and Heroes* (Redleaf Press 1999), will recognize some of the elements that inspired me to write that book:

The Golden Castle

Juan said, "I'm bored, bored, bored."

Marisol said, "Let's play Golden Castles."

Juan said, "I'll be the golden knight."

Marisol said, "I'll be the golden queen."

The Golden Castle has two guard dragons who breathe fire. Aaaaaaah!

Juan said, "Now what do we do?"

Marisol said, "We must say the magic words, *bibbity bobbity boo!*"

"Bibbity bobbity boo!" they shouted.

Suddenly, a golden butterfly named Boo Boo Bitsu flew in the window.

"Help! Help! Rescue me!" he said.

A magic robot monster, who can kill everything and breathe fire, too, caught Boo Boo Bitsu and took him to a secret hiding place in a mountain near the beach.

"Help! Help! Rescue me!" cried Boo Boo Bitsu.

Juan said, "We need powerful magic."

Marisol said, "Guard dragons, help us rescue Boo Boo Bitsu."

The dragons said, "We will call all the other guard dragons." Five hundred guard dragons came.

Juan, Marisol, and the guard dragons ran after the magic robot monster. They met a giant, who said the powerful magic words, *fra qua lego.* But the robot monster didn't die.

"You have to fight with swords," said Juan.

"You have to say different magic words," said Marisol. "Bibbity bobbity boo will do it."

So everyone shouted, "Bibbity bobbity boo!"

The robot monster died, and everyone said, "Hurray!"

They rescued the golden butterfly. "Thank you," said Boo Boo Bitsu. "Now I can change into a golden person. I will be the king."

Then Juan, Marisol, the king, and the guard dragons lived in the Golden Castle forever.

The End

For more about the process of creating stories and books with children, see chapter 5, "Creating Stories for Superhero Play."

Treasure hunts, rainstorms, and volcanoes can provide lots of sensory fun, and kings and castles can elicit wonderful fantasy play, but I find the richest subjects for transitional play come from the animal world. One of my goals each year is to pick one or two animals to study. I get clues from the children about which ones to choose—a girl who loves horses, children who are fascinated with birds, a child who is afraid of dogs. Sometimes everyone gets involved studying one animal, and it becomes the class "totem." Other years a variety of creatures inhabit the room at the same time. We study each one, using books, posters, puzzles, art projects, songs, stuffed animals, and live examples when possible. I try to include information in every learning center. What do they look like? What do they sound like? Where do they live? What do they eat, and how? How do they keep clean? How do they take care of their babies? Where do they sleep, and when? Whenever I ask a question, I also ask the children to compare the animal to themselves. These "child-sized" questions provide more details about the real creature and a better understanding of how they are similar to and different from people, which results in more elaborate and imaginative play.

One animal family, in particular, bridges the real and the fantasy worlds, and that's dinosaurs. Children love to learn dinosaur facts. There are endless educational books, videos, toys, and posters on the subject, and some children want them all. They enjoy knowing more about dinosaurs than the adults do. While it's easy for adults to create popular curriculum about dinosaurs, if you strip away the intellectual veneer, children's fascination with dinosaur play is often about power and fear:

Cheryl, age four: Growl!!!

Teacher: Cheryl, are you angry about something? You look angry.

Cheryl: Oh, no, I'm just a dinosaur. A killer dinosaur. I'm just a killer dinosaur that eats meat people to death. I'm just a killer dinosaur eating all the babies. But I'm not angry, see? I'm just an angry dinosaur. Growl!

Many young children are genuinely afraid that they will meet and be eaten by a T-rex. (Other common worries include dragons, sharks, crocodiles, snakes, spiders, and scorpions.) You can't convince them dinosaurs are extinct, because children have seen them on TV and in the movies. This makes dinosaur play both very attractive and very difficult to keep safe when children become obsessed with it. Dinosaurs show up each year in my classroom, and I support children's interest in them, but I rarely go out of my way to make it a major theme. When I do, the focus is on power and emotions, not just facts.

Animal play works best when you provide costumes and props that help children maintain the image of the animal in their minds. If some new creatures have recently walked (or flown) in your classroom door, here are some simple materials you can provide to support their play. Thanks to the many students and colleagues who contributed their ideas!

★ Mammals need fur. Cut smock shapes out of fake fur, old velour blankets, felt, animal prints, or a variety of earth-colored cloth and slip them over children's heads. These work best when combined with a belt, which helps keep the fur out of the way when walking on all fours. Ask parents for donations, or look in the remnants section of your local fabric store. I prefer fabrics that need no hemming. Avoid cloth that is too scratchy, like burlap. While fur is fun, children won't wear it on a hot day for long.

★ For tails, use about 3 feet of string, cloth, elastic, or shoelace as a waist belt, then tie a tail of cloth or yarn to the back. Tails get in the way if they are more than 18 inches long. Adding Velcro at the ends of the belt makes it easier for children to use without adult help. The material and length of the tail piece will depend on the kind of animal you're outfitting. Yarn, in shades of brown, black, yellow, and white, works well for a variety of animals. Strips of cloth or soft ribbon give a different texture. For a thicker tail, braid cloth strips or use thick, soft rope.

For some animals, only a stuffed tail will do. Child-size pantyhose or knee-high socks provide a good casing. If you have someone who is willing to sew, you can make a casing out of the same material you used for the furs. Stuff with cotton, rags, socks, or even newsprint. Leave enough room at the end to tie off and attach to a belt. A light-colored mesh bag or a square of white sheet fabric filled with cotton or polyester fill makes a good rabbit tail.

★ Ear shapes can be attached to headbands, hair clips, or hats. You can buy inexpensive headbands, make them from stretchy fabric, or make them from cloth strips that tie or Velcro together. Thick fabrics and felts or thinner fabrics that are rolled and then cut make the best ears. Make them any shape you want, but if they are too long, they will droop! Painting them with diluted white glue will help. The best ears are sewn on to the headbands, of course, but in a pinch I've stapled them together. Make sure the staple points face away from the child's skin.

★ You will have to use your judgment about masks. Children love to make them, but not many preschoolers will wear them for long. They get in the way of play, and are soon discarded. Some young children are afraid of them, because they don't understand that the person underneath hasn't really changed. I find that masks work for kindergarten ages and up; I prefer to use face paints with preschoolers. Children can make simple masks by cutting eye holes in wide strips of cloth, then decorating them with markers, fabric paints, and glue-on jewels. They can also incorporate ears into their mask design. This is a great group design problem for elementary ages—let them figure out how to get the eyes, ears, and noses in the right place.

★ Claws, teeth, and horns are props I avoid introducing to preschoolers. Still, every year, somebody in my class figures out how to put pen tops on their fingers to make claws. Soon, there's growling and howling and clawing at people's faces. Adding horns or other sharp elements to animal play tends to make it noisy and aggressive, and some children can't control themselves. Perhaps these would work in a small group, but I usually don't introduce them into my classroom, except for an occasional gentle unicorn or reindeer, like Susie, age five:

> *I'm a teeny tiny unicorn, as teeny as dust. I can't even walk. I have a poky, poky horn, and it's as little as dust too. And my hooves, teeny as dust! And I'm very, very fuzzy. Even the fuzz is teeny as dust!*

Here are additional props and activities I've used to set up curriculum for specific animals:

★ The horse is one of my favorite animal spirits to visit the classroom. Horses are powerful and graceful, and they run with a variety of rhythms. Yarn tails and felt ears are all they need, but children who really know horses demand more—like manes, shoes, and other accessories. For the mane, I've attached a fur or fringed cloth strip between the headband that holds the ears and the belt that holds the tail. (One child insisted I use a bright orange fur strip and claimed it was made of fire. When she danced a fire dance, everyone knew it was true.)

Children love experimenting to find shoes that make the perfect horse noise. Wood blocks with handholds attached work well on a sidewalk, especially if you hammer some nails in them. Wood sticks can make a good sound, but they turn into guns quite easily. If you want to create horseshoe prints in sand or mud, roll and bend aluminum foil and glue them onto wood blocks.

Most pretend horses prefer to run wild, but some are willing to work, so hitch them up singly or in teams to wagons, sleds, boxes, or old tires. If it's snowing, don't forget the jingle bells. Be sure nothing goes around children's necks.

Horses live in stables, corrals, or barns. Make them out of wood barriers, ropes with blankets over them, chairs, or sawhorses. If you don't mind turning over some tables, you can make stalls by wrapping yarn or cloth around the legs to cover three sides. Add some fresh hay covered with a sheet, and put your horses to bed.

Children like to be horses, but they also like to pretend to ride them. I've used real saddles when I can, but I've also used various configurations of blankets rolled up and tied. For a base, I've used hay bales, low sawhorses and benches, and sections of thick cardboard concrete-form tubing (available at most lumber yards; the tubing must be stabilized with wood blocks). One caution—horse-riding play can bring out cowboy and Indian stereotypes.

Other horse props and activities my staff has used include a barn made of branches tied together, a racetrack with jumps, and feed sacks. We created a slow-motion horse dance at circle, where the children were able to rear up and paw at each other without hurting each other, and a horse hide-and-seek game. A pony visited, and everyone got to brush it and feed it. Pictures of the visit, horseshoes, and horse hair went into a science display. For children who preferred playing with miniature horses, we made a set of stalls for the block area out of shoeboxes and used strips of cloth and yarn for bedding.

Occasionally, horses want to sprout horns and become gentle unicorns or reindeer, my one exception to the "no horns" rule. I even had one child-horse who loved mythology and grew wings. Time to bring out the magic wands!

★ No matter what I do, my classroom always seems to end up full of dogs and puppies. Some like their ears long and floppy, some like them short and pointy. Some like to be led around on leashes—real ones, or ones made from string or cloth. Be sure your puppies tie their leashes to their waists or wrists, not around their necks.

Dogs like to do tricks—rolling over, shaking hands, fetching sticks, and jumping through hoops. They like to chew bones and bury them. I make bones out of short pieces of white plastic pipe, with plastic caps glued on the ends. Don't forget to wash them frequently. Dogs also like to sleep on big pillows or in big baskets, and they like to hang out in doghouses under tables, in boxes, and below the climbing structure.

Sometimes dogs turn into foxes, wolves, or coyotes, living in dens and caves. As one five-year-old puppy named Susan told me, "Bad magic turned me into a baby wild wolf." I particularly love coyotes because there are so many coyote stories to read, but you should check with your neighbors to see if they mind the howling.

★ I love cats, but cats and kittens refuse to learn tricks. They sleep and wash themselves a lot, which doesn't appeal to preschoolers for long periods, so they often have nothing to do but screech and fight. But they're a great animal for children who love to climb. Cats like painted whiskers on their faces, wear bells on their wrists or in their hair, and play with balls of yarn. Old shoulder pads make perfect cat ears! Some cats turn into wilder cousins that can be hard to control, so let them in at your own risk. For an example, see the story called "Leopards, Lions, and Tigers" in chapter 7, "Working with Families and Staff."

★ Birds need to fly, whether they're hummingbirds or hawks, so make bird wings. I use one or more fringed layers of silky cloth, doubled over at the top and sewn to make arm tubes. Cut them short enough that the birds don't trip on themselves when their wings are at their sides. I set up jumping ramps that lead to mats or big pillows so the birds can experiment with flight.

Birds also need nests. I've made them out of pillows, or low boxes filled with hay. My favorite, though, is to use tires, cover them with a blanket, and fill them with dried leaves. Just the right place to keep your eggs.

Eggs? I've got a variety of plastic and wooden ones, including the kind that hold pantyhose. Or try crumpling newspaper into egg shapes and covering them with masking tape. Elementary children can use balloons to make papier-mâché eggs. I let older preschoolers paint round rocks to carry around and sit on—there is nothing sweeter than seeing a group of boys and girls wearing wings and chirping away while they sit in tires on their painted rock eggs, occasionally checking to see if they have hatched.

One of the best parts of bird play is studying real birds. Children can do a tremendous amount of science and art with feathers, bird feeders, eggs, and nests, and much can be done by looking out your window—most schools have several varieties of birds in their immediate environment. I know I've been successful when my young birds are looking out the window, carefully copying the movements and songs of a bird nearby.

★ Squirrels and mice are very busy and mischievous. They like to hide treasures, chew food quickly using only their front teeth, and pop out of holes. Real acorns or other nuts are a plus, especially if you spray-paint them gold. You can also use beads and small pieces of wood, but nothing children can choke on. Crackers and apple slices make a perfect squirrel or mouse snack. Sometimes, I let them eat it in their trees. Groups of chairs make fine trees or burrows, along with barely-big-enough cardboard boxes, pieces of concrete-form tubing, stacks of tires, or spaces in the climbing structure.

★ I've only had beavers in my classroom once. We had some great play with mud, water, and sticks that year. One problem I never solved: How do you make a beaver tail that children can really slap on water?

Providing Props and Play Spaces that Inspire Superhero Play

Once children move into superhero play, planning environments to support it becomes more complex. To support early dramatic play, teachers provide materials that help children imitate real people, animals, and objects. Some of these characters can easily turn into superhero figures: firefighters, airplane pilots, and cats can develop super abilities without much trouble. For the most part, though, the roles and props from earlier play are abandoned when children move into superhero play. Superheroes require new kinds of materials, because the roles and tools they use are no longer tied into real people and objects. They are symbols, such as magic wands, potions, capes, power bracelets, and imaginary weapons, that allow children to think about their feelings and their desires for power, control, and connection.

These new materials can bring up adult concerns that earlier play avoids. Most superhero play props are clearly fantasy objects, but guns have both fantasy and real uses. Guns appear widely in the media as symbols of authority and fear, so children naturally turn to them in their play. But guns also have power in the real world that can be destructive. Parents and teachers worry that children who use guns to represent power are unknowingly becoming desensitized to this violence. I have found that I can't completely erase these images from children's minds or stop them from wanting to use them as powerful icons. In fact, banning them often increases this desire. I have been more successful when I provide them with props and play opportunities that expand their idea of what is powerful.

When I'm looking for alternatives for children to use as the focus of superhero play, I like to use materials that borrow their strength from nature. That way, I can tie some actual science curriculum into the play. Some things shine, with a little bit of the sun's magic: jewels, silky cloth, spangles, metal buttons, shiny metal or plastic shapes, and objects painted with gold or silver or decorated with glitter. Others are also associated with the sky: feathers, rainbows, wings, and star, moon, snowflake, or lightning shapes. Some come from the earth: bones, dried flowers or moss, gourd rattles, herb sachets, pieces of fake fur, and polished rocks, clay beads, or wood. Others are related to the water: shells, coral, driftwood, and shark teeth.

Teachers can use these materials to create new props, or let children make their own. Here are some possibilities:

★ I've made power bracelets out of stretch trim fabrics, beads, and shells. If you don't want to do the sewing, many thrift stores have lots of cheap plastic and metal bracelets available. Get lots of them—once they catch on, children like to wear multiple bracelets on their wrists and ankles.

★ Scarves can be used in many ways. Try a variety of silky, fancy fabrics. Add Velcro closures to the corners if you know someone who will sew them on. They can be used as capes, skirts, headbands, belts, and even super-diapers! Oversized, ornate shirts can also be a useful part of a superhero costume.

★ Hats, baseball caps, headbands, hair barrettes, or paper crowns can be decorated with jewels, glitter glue, and feathers.

★ Wands can be made from decorated branches, dowels, or plastic rods, but I only give these hard materials to groups that won't use them as swords. For others, I'll try rolled-up colored papers, twisted pipe cleaners, or pieces of foam. The younger the child, the shorter the wand. Older children like to have stars on the ends.

★ Badges and medals come in handy for rewarding bravery and compassion. They can be made out of juice can or jar lids, thick cardboard shapes, or large poker chips. Drill or punch holes in them, spray paint them silver or gold if you wish, then tie them onto ribbons, yarn, or strips of decorative cloth.

★ Magic buttons can be pushed at any time to make a wish come true. A button, bottle cap, or other small object can be glued to a small decorated piece of wood or cardboard for a pocket-sized version, or to something larger for a shared magic button in the dramatic play area.

★ Children like to carry miscellaneous magic objects, such as painted or polished rocks and twigs, old keys, coins, decorated thread spools, old watches, or safe pieces of broken machinery.

★ An old cell phone is an essential tool for any modern superhero, especially if it is spray painted gold.

★ There are many magical ways to carry and hide power symbols. Everyday objects gain power if they are associated with the grown-up world, like wallets, purses, backpacks, and belly bags. You can also make paper or cloth pouches, attach them to old belts or ties, and let children wear them around their waists or over their shoulders. Some children prefer to have their magic items taped directly onto their clothes or bodies.

This is what children said after making magic buttons out of wood, buttons, glitter, fake jewels, and tissue paper. They were asked, "What happens when you press your magic button?"

"When my mommy presses the gold jewel it will lock her in the bathroom. When she presses the silver jewel she will get a new table." — *Tobie, age three*

"When Mama presses this button she'll never have to work again and she'll stay home and raise our duck." —*Sylvia, age four*

"When my dad and mom press this button, they'll get infinity dollars and they can buy anything." —*Marc, age five*

"The red button makes me go to the field. The blue button is for making me apologize. The clear button is for making my mom come before school is over." —*Barbara, age four*

"When Mama presses this button, she'll give me a hug." —*Claire, age three*

"This one is special. It makes you have another baby." —*Rudy, age five*

These superhero props are all in the category of small child-moveable materials. What kind of play spaces work for superhero play? Since superhero play is often done on the run, it requires space, preferably with some large motor activities in it. Climbing structures or wide-open grass areas are often the sites for this play. Less active superhero games, like mixing potions in the sandbox, don't take up as much room. But I find that most superheroes like to have a hideout—a cave, den, rocket ship, or house. I have created these home bases below and on top of climbing structures, under tables, on top of overturned tables, and inside cabinets, playhouses, and tents. They work best if they are a combination of built-in or teacher-moveable equipment with added child-moveable elements that children can use to change the space—cardboard boxes, large outdoor blocks, blankets, sheets, or big pillows. Some games also need a place for bad guys, either another hideout or a jail.

Hideouts have two advantages. The first is that they provide a quieter place within an active game, a "no chase" zone where children can rest, negotiate the rules and storylines that govern the game, and make big plans. The second is that they provide a place for teachers to set up curriculum that can broaden the scope of the game. I have used superhero hideouts as a protected place to put simple art materials, board books, sensory tables, puppet theaters, table blocks, and even doll beds. Materials that superheroes wouldn't touch in other learning centers can become part of their story when they are thoughtfully introduced into their hideouts.

You can't just plunk new materials like these in the middle of a game and expect them to work, especially in superhero play, where they are competing with guns and other media-generated symbols of power that already have a hold on children's imaginations. Everyone understands these commercial images, with little need for conversation or negotiation. Funny bracelets and overturned tables have no clout until these props and spaces are given a shared meaning that imbues them with power. The best way to do this is to connect the materials to a superhero story the children help create. The next chapter, "Creating Stories for Superhero Play," will go into more details.

STORIES FROM THE CLASSROOM

The Heroines and Heroes Cave

One of my favorite dramatic play setups for superhero play is the "Heroines and Heroes Cave." I have used it for many years, and each year the children create new materials, powers, and stories to fill it. The idea for it developed out of one child's play. Three-year-old Carlos was a bat ("But not Batman," he insisted) who swooped around the playground in a cape, sometimes stealing toys, and sometimes trying to help others, even when they didn't want to be helped. He then flew behind the bookshelf or the couch and curled up in his cave to suck his thumb.

More children began wearing capes and making caves, behind shelves and under tables, and turning into animals, monsters, and superheroes. They hoarded puzzles, blocks, paper, and anything else they could carry into their dens. The feeling of community my staff was trying to encourage was being overshadowed by a distrustful and competitive tone.

We decided to set up a communal cave. We emptied out a low storage area that was big enough for three or four children to crawl inside. We took off the doors, padded the wood at the top of the entrance, threw in a piece of carpet, and decorated the walls with a star-covered cloth a parent had donated.

Shelly, one of the four-year-olds, said, "It needs rocks." So we brought out earth-toned papers and everyone cut and decorated rock shapes. The children taped them all around the cave entrance. I made a sign that said, "Heroines and Heroes Cave."

The cave was an immediate hit, and the children worked cooperatively to create it, but the play that happened in it was still about robbing, tricking, and bothering others. I decided to enlist Saul and Zora, flannelboard characters that I had been using all year at circle time to help me tell stories, talk about feelings, teach lessons, and introduce new curriculum.

I made a felt version of the cave, including an archway of rocks and a sign that said "Heroines and Heroes Cave" and covered the edge of the flannelboard. I brought everything to circle on a tray. After a song and a look at the weather, I put the cave on the flannelboard, held up Pic Pac, the flannelboard cat, and placed him at the top of a brown and green felt tree.

"Help! Meow! Rescue me!" I said. "Oh, no, Pic Pac is stuck in the tree! What should we do?"

Fifteen preschoolers watched with wide eyes. Shelly raised her hand. "She can't climb down. My cat did that. We had to get a ladder."

"How should I reach her?" I asked.

Another four-year-old said, "Saul and Zora can climb up and get her down. Hurry!"

I took the two flannelboard characters, Saul and Zora, and placed them on the board.

"They don't have a ladder," I said. "All they have are their new power belts." I picked up two felt strips that I had decorated with stick-on jewels and put them around Saul and Zora's neck.

"Where did they get them?" someone asked. "What do they do?"

"I made them, but you'll have to decide what they do."

Carlos stood up. "They can fly! Those are magic flying belts. They can fly up and get Pic Pac."

"Well, let's try it," I said. "Everybody pretend to put on a magic flying belt." All the children pretended to buckle up. "Now fly!" I said, and everyone stretched out their arms and flew.

"I got Pic Pac!" several children claimed. "I saved her!"

"No, I did," Carlos said. He looked ready to fight.

"Hold on," I said, "we all have to work together to help Zora and Saul. They're the ones who will rescue Pic Pac. Let's try again. Keep flying!"

I held Zora and Saul and flew them around the room. Everyone followed, back to the block area where circle time was held. Zora and Saul grabbed

Pic Pac and set her down on the ground. "Pic Pac is safe," I said. "He says 'Thank you' for rescuing him."

"Hooray!" Fifteen children jumped and wiggled with excitement.

I waited for everyone to find a seat. "I made magic belts for Zora and Saul, but I don't have belts for all of you," I said. "I do have some fancy cloth and jewels to make bracelets, though. If you would like to make your own magic bracelet after snack, come to the art area."

Circle time was over. I moved the flannelboard and all its components into the "Heroines and Heroes Cave," so children could re-create the story or make up new ones after snack.

After circle, about half the children wanted to make bracelets. They glued strips of cloth together and decorated them with jewels, gold and silver dots, and buttons. As they made their bracelets, one of the aides wrote down their ideas for what the bracelets could do. She had to set clear rules for the discussion, because children started arguing about whose answer was right. Here is the list she made:

What My Power Bracelet Can Do
- My bracelet lets me see my daddy wherever he is.
- I can fly across the lake and ocean to the North Pole.
- My bracelet lets me fly up and rescue people who are stuck on top of mountains and on airplanes before they crash.
- I kill monsters. The energy surges out and blinds them and kills them.
- I use my power bracelet when I am too sad.
- Mine makes a little noise and glows. That's all.
- My power bracelet has the power of kung fu inside.
- This is a secret walkie-talkie. I can talk to anybody else who wears one.

We had a hard time convincing some of the children to wait until the next day for their bracelets to dry. In the meantime, we could hear children in the cave debating what kind of rescue they should perform, a welcome change from the usual discussion of whose toys they would steal.

The next day, many of the children put on their power bracelets. Others wanted to make one, and some wanted a second or third. "I need another one to take home in case my cat goes up in the tree again," said Shelly. There were several fights about what the bracelets could do.

I brought Pic Pac, Saul, and Zora back to circle. "Pic Pac wants to play another rescue game, but she heard you fighting about what the power bracelets could do. She's worried that she'll get hurt if you don't decide together. She wants to know what power people can use when they wear the bracelets."

The circle erupted in heated debates. Children were yelling and shaking fists. I was sure I had lost control of the situation.

"Meow. Help! Rescue me!" I whispered as I walked around the circle holding Pic Pac high in the air. "Help! I need help!"

The children gradually calmed down, although no one sat down. "Everyone is getting so angry, and I need your help. I'll come to each of you and you can tell me what power your bracelet gives you, then I'll tell you which one will work to help me. Raise your hand if you have an idea."

I carried Pic Pac and held her up to each child who wanted to speak. Some wanted to fly, some wanted super strength. Carlos said his bracelet let him make people who were sick get well right away.

I decided to support Carlos. I knew why he had chosen what he did. His older brother had been in and out of the hospital for the past year.

"Pic Pac says that she is getting so very sick, and she needs everyone to work together to get her to the hospital and make her feel better."

After we all agreed, everyone held their bracelets in the air and said, "Get better, Pic Pac," and Pic Pac felt a whole lot better.

Over the next few days, we turned an outdoor shady spot into a hospital, with cots, blankets, medical supplies, and Red Cross shirts. The school wagons became ambulances, each with a nap cot "stretcher." As children got hurt in imagined accidents, a call would go out for one of the super-heroes waiting in the Heroines and Heroes Cave. A runner would come to the door and speak into a walkie-talkie, then a superhero would zoom out (we told the children we would make an exception to our usual "no running indoors" rule) with his or her power bracelet held high to lead an ambulance crew across the playground with sirens blaring. Everyone learned to pull over to the side when an ambulance was coming through. Under adult supervision, a group of children would lift the victim onto the stretcher, and the stretcher would be lifted onto the ambulance. Back at the hospital, other superheroes waited with bandages, braces, medicine, lots of shots, and bracelets with healing powers. Carlos was often the superhero and head doctor.

We also invited visitors into the classroom to keep the play grounded in some realistic curriculum. We arranged for an ambulance to visit. Family members came in to discuss their work: a mother who was a doctor, an older brother who was a lifeguard, a father who helped with marine animal rescues.

The children created new power symbols as they needed them. Some made power necklaces out of beads with a variety of powers, some decorated smooth rocks. Sally picked out a piece of yellow ribbon and declared it to be a golden rope that she could use to rescue cats from trees.

After a month, there was little sign of the robber mentality that had threatened to poison the classroom atmosphere. Carlos, the bat child, was no longer hiding behind the couch sucking his thumb, but was right in the middle of the play. Almost everyone in the classroom was participating and enjoying the games. Everyone, I decided, except another one of my flannelboard characters, Juana.

Juana, like all the other characters, had her own story. She loved to garden, had a pet snake, liked to dress up and paint her nails, and often decorated her wheelchair with flags. I pretended that Juana was upset, and helped her speak about it at circle time.

"Everyone is playing in the new cave, but I can't because my wheelchair doesn't fit. It's not fair!"

"Not fair!" some of the children grumbled.

"We should make the cave bigger," said a five-year-old. "We could use real rocks. We could use our magic rocks."

"Yeah!" everyone said.

"I'm not sure that would be safe," I said. "What else could we use?"

"Metal!"

"Big boxes!"

"Windows!"

"Sorry, no glass," I said.

"Wood!"

"Hammers and nails and wood!"

"Yes!" others shouted. "We'll make a super cave!"

Over the next few days, two carpenter parents brought in a pile of wood strips. The staff gathered cardboard boxes. Children drew pictures of what they thought the cave should look like. Most of them envisioned structures that were several stories high and big enough for a small department store.

The staff chose a simpler design, 5 feet high and 4 feet square. Cardboard walls would cover a frame of wood strips that were screwed together. The structure would attach to the mouth of the existing cave.

We set up a construction zone with orange cones, safety barriers, and hard hats. Adults helped children measure and cut the wood at the outdoor carpentry bench. Teachers cut the cardboard to size. Staff and volunteer parents worked one-on-one with children to screw the framework together and staple the cardboard to the frame. The children moved their paper-rock decorations to the front, and drew new designs directly on the cardboard walls with markers and paint.

"These are magic drawings. They should have magic words," a child said.

"Like what?" I said.

"Like abracadabra. Words like that."

At circle time, we made a list of magic words:

- Abracadabra
- Macko
- Kalamazoo
- Dinosaur-a Grabba
- Ababanana
- Pooh Pooh
- Skateboard
- Inspector Gadget

- Sharkteeth Horrible
- Agracadagger

We wrote each one on a paper strip and children taped them to the cave. We added strips with each child's name.

When it was done, we had an end of the day "New, Improved Heroes and Heroines Cave Grand Opening Tea Party." All the families were invited. I borrowed a wheelchair and brought it to the festivities.

"We have to make sure it fits," I said.

The children helped me put Juana and the other characters on the flannelboard to watch. A family member sat in the chair, and two children helped wheel her into the cave.

"It fits!" the children shouted. "Hooray! Now Juana can play the game! We're heroines and heroes!"

The staff had made special medals for the event. Everyone who wanted a medal got one, and we partied straight through lunch.

The Heroines and Heroes Cave and the bracelets and other objects we created didn't become powerful just because they were made with fancy materials. The staff and children had to work together to bring the props to life and give them an aura of authority, mystery, and magic. In the process, the staff learned what was important to the children, and got to tie in literacy and math activities to their interests. And the children learned an important lesson in how to be heroes and heroines—helping others when something is unfair.

CHAPTER 5

Creating Stories for Superhero Play

Darian, age three:
Everybody run!

Chela, age five:
No, stop. What
are we playing?

Darian: Bad guys.

Chela: I know, but what are the bad
guys supposed to do in this game?

Darian: They run. They shoot everybody.

Chela: That's boring.

AS CHILDREN'S SUPERHERO PLAY becomes more complex, the storyline that guides the play becomes more important to the success of the game. Three-year-olds, like Darian, don't mind playing a chase game with a vague purpose, but older fours and fives, like Chela, have bigger needs. They want to be part of a team, with roles that interact and depend on each other. They want powerful actions and magical props that everyone in the game understands. Before they can start having fun, they have to figure out at least the beginnings of a shared story. Then they can fill in the details as they play.

Understanding how to make up and play out a story is a learned skill. Some children come to preschool knowing a lot about this process, while others have little conception of what a story is. Very few preschoolers know how to create a story with a group of peers. Teachers can encourage creative storytelling by

- ★ Being aware of the influences on children's storytelling
- ★ Understanding how children's play stories develop
- ★ Introducing written storytelling to children
- ★ Creating books from children's stories
- ★ Using dolls, puppets, and flannelboard characters
- ★ Creating theater from children's play
- ★ Transforming media characters into new stories

Being Aware of the Influences on Children's Storytelling

The stories children tell grow out of the ones they have been exposed to at home and at school. The more stories a child has heard, the better intuitive understanding they will have of storytelling. The source and style of these stories varies from culture to culture and family to family. Some rely on oral narratives, without reference to any written text. These stories have been used to educate children to the shared history, mythology, and values of their culture for much of human history. In many cultures, this style of storytelling has been expanded into more formal theater, which combines the spoken word with role playing. Today, most American children also absorb hours of dramatic storytelling through movies and television. Children's dramatic play has a format similar to theater.

Written storytelling has a much shorter history. It's only in the past few hundred years that any but the wealthiest children have been read to from books, starting with adult religious texts, and then from collections of lessons, fables, and folktales. The mainstay of the contemporary American preschool, the picture book, first appeared in the seventeenth century, but didn't become widely available until the end of the 1800s.

Picture books have helped build the widely accepted belief in the United States that all children should learn to read. They are now used as a way to transition children into reading on their own.

Each of these ways of telling stories has its own process and structure. When children listen to oral stories, they have to use their imaginations to stay connected to the storyteller's ideas and turn what they hear into mental pictures. The storyteller and the listener have to work together to create the visual and emotional content. Visual storytelling is a more passive process, particularly with the hyperrealism of today's computer-generated special effects. There is no real relationship created between the child and the storyteller, and the fast pace of editing on many TV shows does not allow children time to think about and understand what they are seeing. TV stories are also disrupted and broken up by an impersonal element not found in other storytelling modes—advertisements. Written stories for young children, on the other hand, depend on an older person who takes the time to translate what is on the page into the spoken word. Picture books combine oral, written, and visual storytelling traditions into a unique format, although with the constant invention of new printing technologies over the last fifty years, the visual element in picture books has taken on a larger and larger role.

One new format of storytelling is emerging today: Computers allow children to alter stories by choosing from multiple plot options and visual elements. They will undoubtedly change storytelling for children in ways no one has conceived.

Yet with all these differences, there are still basic elements common to all stories that children learn about at an early age. Most stories have a logical sequence that starts by introducing characters and setting up a problem. The middle of the story shows the characters' attempts to solve it, and the ending releases the story's tension by showing how the problem gets worked out, with the characters experiencing some growth or learning in the process. Along the way, the listener or viewer expects to make emotional connections to the characters and plot, through humor, sadness, fear, or joy. Most people develop an expectation for this storytelling flow as toddlers.

Children come to our classrooms with a wide variation in their experience with storytelling formats and their ability to use them in their play. Some families read young children long stories from chapter books or collections of fairy tales and mythologies that can last for weeks. Some have extensive libraries of picture books, or borrow them from libraries, and read several a day. A few families also cherish oral storytelling, in person, on audiotape, or on the radio.

Most teachers report, though, that the biggest influences on the stories American children use in their superhero play are the visual media—TV, videos, and movies. Many children who come to our classrooms have never been read to. Teachers of young children have an obligation to introduce these children to oral and written storytelling. Superhero play provides an excellent opportunity for teachers to get their students interested in listening, reading, and writing, because the stories children use in their play are so exciting to them.

One concern comes up repeatedly in my discussions with parents and teachers about the dominance of visual storytelling: the emphasis on violence in the play that follows. One reason to read picture books to young children is that they have, for the most part, resisted the temptation of weapons and violence. Picture books have little reason to depend on images of guns, the way many visual media productions do. They engage children by giving them time to observe, think, ask questions, and interact with the storyteller.

While teachers' concerns about violence in the media are legitimate, it's important to keep them in perspective. Violence has always had a prominent place in drama and literature, both for children and for adults. A master storyteller can use violent action, balanced with moments of clever thinking, emotional insight, and heroic deeds, to teach valuable lessons about emotions, power, good and evil, life and death, and creation and destruction. Mythologies and children's tales from around the world are filled with such images. While some adults condemn any portrayal of violence for children, we can't pretend it doesn't exist, or assume that children will never encounter it, wonder about it, or have violent thoughts. Violence is real; children will use it in their stories, and need help thinking about it. Good storytelling raises our awareness of ideas and emotions, even difficult ones; poor storytelling leaves us numb.

Understanding How Children's Play Stories Develop

As children get older and gain experience listening to and creating stories, their play narratives develop more continuity and structure. Children learn to compromise and cooperate within a group to craft a storyline for a game. Superhero narratives need several elements to succeed in group play. There must be powerful characters that children can identify with. At least one, and usually more, have to be considered good guys or heroes that possess superhuman abilities or props. There must be a problem or fear the characters overcome in ways that require physical skill, bravery, magic, or clear thinking. Very often, this involves defeating a villain and coming to the aid of a victim. And there is usually some recognition of the hero by other characters at the end of the story.

Children's stories usually start out as simple statements of fact, or stream-of-consciousness meanderings. Take, for example, this story from two-and-a-half-year-old Victoria:

> *I'm making Boxman. Once I climbed the roof and a monster kicked me off the roof and I was drowning in the ocean. I was here and then over there and over there and over the world to New York and China's ocean.*

When toddlers or young preschoolers play together, each child often has a different story line in mind:

> *Jim, age two: I'm cooking the eggs. Here's your tortilla, man. (Hands a plate to Ramone.)*
>
> *Ramone, age three: I'm flying to the mountains, goodbye. It's a bat car. (Uses the plate as a steering wheel.)*
>
> *Jim: Was that so delicious, baby? Here's another one.*

But as children gain experience, their play narratives start showing more storytelling elements, as in this dictated story by three-and-a-half-year-old Joseph:

> *There was once a monster who hated mouses. Every time he was about to go to sleep he set his gun and while he was watching no mouses came. He trapped no mouses. And God told him, "The reason you are trapping no mouses is because there are no mouses around here to be trapped." But then one day, to his surprise, he found that he really was trapping mouses. So he sent a warship to have a big battle until God told him, "Do not have a battle." So he became friends with the mouses, and that's the end.*

As they mature, children start working together to create story ideas and characters. Successfully creating a story together is one way children know they are friends:

Robert, age four: I'm a superhero! Who will be the mother?

Leana, age five: I'm the mother!

Robert: How come?

Leana: Because I'm invisible. And because I'm an alien. And because I have magic hats. And because I can read.

Robert: Hello, Mother!

Leana: Hello. Are you my friend now?

As children spend more time listening to each other's ideas, their stories start to overlap and build on each other. Children work out some of the story elements in groups as they play. Notice the way the children in this next scenario regularly check in with each other with the question, "Right?"

Lana, age four: (Holding squished mint in a dish) Here guys. Here's your medicine. This is the wake-up magic, right?

Roanne, age five: This is the wake-up magic. This is the shot. You press on something here, right? On their tummy. This coats it so it doesn't hurt, then we put the shot on.

Millie, age four: You're the one that does it. The boy is kind of really sick. There's a boy and a girl, so we're healing them.

Roanne: And we have to tell them what we are. We're fairies, right?

Lana: They're kind of sick, but we're healing them up.

Millie: Yes, we're the fairies that heal.

The stories become more sophisticated as children get used to having more elements of storytelling — setting the scene, introducing characters, creating suspense and conflict, and resolving the conflict through heroic action. Older children may create several problems to solve in the same story:

Celia, age five: Get on the spaceship, quick! It's running, it's leaving the ground. Get away from the hot lava! Blast out! Power! Power! We're going twice power speed!

Martine, age five: This is our spaceship. This is our house that floats in space, and we can do tricks in it. It has a place to eat, and a bathroom, and a place to pump gas. Here's the guns, but we don't need them. We have superpowers! And there are pictures of Pokemon— Pikachu, Ash, and some others too.

Celia: The spaceship is out in space and someone gets lost, right? If you get lost we have some long hoses to save you. And if you get killed by a terrible monster, if the terrible monster bites you, then the magic witch will save you. We have magic powers, too, so we can save you if you die.

Sal, age four: Hooray, we're the rescue party! But watch out for the hot lava.

Martine: Oh, no! The map fell into the Earth. But we're not afraid. We can fly, right?

All: We can fly! We can fly!

When I see children using a cooperative storytelling process in their play, I know they are ready to create more formal stories in written form.

Introducing Written Storytelling to Children

How can a teacher get started helping children create new play stories? First, by setting up an environment that is rich in both print and oral storytelling, and reading, reading, reading. For some children, your classroom will provide their primary exposure to stories not told by a TV. Take the time to ask questions as you read, such as, "What do you think should happen next?" and "Why do you think she did that?" Let children interrupt with their ideas and opinions. Be prepared to cheerfully read the same book over and over, even when you are sick of it. Let children help you select the books that will go on your shelves. Take them to the library to pick out books that support your current curriculum themes.

Here are some picture books with themes that fit in well with children's superhero play:

Carlson, Nancy C. *There's a Big, Beautiful World Out There.* New York: Viking, 2002.

Carlsson-Paige, Nancy. *Best Day of the Week.* St. Paul, Redleaf Press, 1998.

Cocca-Leffler, Maryann. *Bravery Soup.* Morton Grove, IL: Albert Whitman, 2002.

de Paola, Tomie. *Bill and Pete to the Rescue.* New York: Puffin, 2001.

de Paola, Tomie. *The Knight and the Dragon.* New York: Putnam, 1980.

Graham, Bob. *Max.* Cambridge, MA: Candlewick, 2000.

Greco, Francesca. *Gideon.* New York: Star Bright Books, 2003.

Hayles, Marsha. *He Saves the Day.* New York: Putnam, 2002.

Henkes, Kevin. *Sheila Rae, the Brave.* New York: Greenwillow, 1996.

Herrera, Juan Felipe. *Super Cilantro Girl.* San Francisco: Children's Book Press, 2003.

Hoffman, Eric. *Heroines and Heroes.* St. Paul: Redleaf Press, 1999.

Hoffman, Eric. *No Fair to Tigers.* St. Paul: Redleaf Press, 1999.

Hoffman, Eric. *Play Lady.* St. Paul: Redleaf Press, 1999.

MacLean, Christine Kole. *Even Firefighters Hug Their Moms.* New York: Dutton, 2002.

Martin, Rafe. *The Brave Little Parrot.* New York: Putnam, 1998.

Munsch, Robert N. *Paper Bag Princess.* Willowdale, ON, Canada: Annick Press, 1988.

Osborne, Mary Pope. *New York's Bravest.* New York, Knopf, 2002.

Roberts, Bethany. *Rosie to the Rescue.* New York: Henry Holt, 2003.

Rohmann, Eric. *My Friend Rabbit.* Brookfield, CT: Millbrook, 2002.

Schuch, Steve. *A Symphony of Whales.* San Diego: Harcourt, 1999.

Sierra, Judy. *Preschool to the Rescue.* New York: Gulliver Books, 2001.

Waber, Bernard. *Courage.* Boston, Houghton Mifflin, 2002.

Whatley, Bruce. *Captain Pajamas: Defender of the Universe.* New York: HarperCollins, 2000.

Zakarin, Deborah Mostow. *Grandpa Lets Me Be Me.* New York: Grosset and Dunlop, 2002.

Reading to children regularly improves their chances of learning to read. The other strategy that can help tremendously is to watch, listen, and write. Writing down children's words teaches them that anything they say can be written, saved, and read back. That may seem obvious to adults, but it is a revelation to young children. I like to hang observation clipboards throughout my classroom and playground so my staff will always have a place nearby to write down conversations or document children's activities. Sometimes they can copy conversations word for word; sometimes they have to re-create them as best they can later on. Many of the examples used throughout this book were taken from these clipboards.

When adults use the clipboards regularly, it doesn't take long for the children to get involved. They want to know what the teachers are up to. I always ask if children want me to read their words, and then I ask, "Do you want me to write anything else?" Soon, the children aren't waiting for the staff. They come up and say, "Write this down." The observation boards become dictation boards. Some years, children have wanted their own boards to write on, so I have hung new ones at child level; these are much more attractive to write on than the paper we put out on the shelves in the art area, because they imitate an adult activity. Most years, I also create individual notebooks for children to draw and write in anytime they want or dictate words for an adult to write. At that point, the dictation process usually takes on a life of its own. Some children will want you to write down their words every day.

Observations and dictations allow my staff to support children's storytelling in several ways. By reading through them regularly, we can

★ Get a better idea of the story lines that are important to the children and will hold their attention
★ Plan ways to support these story lines with props, art projects, and other curriculum projects
★ Select books to read that complement the plots or characters children are using, to see if children will incorporate them into their play
★ Bring children's ideas to circle time and play them out with flannelboard characters, puppets, and dolls, then ask what the children want to add
★ Form questions that lead to group lists and poems

Here are examples of a group list and poem based on what teachers observed in children's play. In the first one, children were fascinated by the idea of one object transforming into another, an attribute built into many toys. After discussing what the word *transform* means with a group of three- and four-year-olds, the teacher posed the question, "What else would you like to know about transforming?" Notice that the first child's response set the form for all the answers that followed. Here is the list they created:

What We Want to Know about Transforming
How can a doggie be a bubble?
How can a heart be a slide?
How can a monster be a prince?
How can a ladybug be a forest?
How can a bat be a flower?

How can a kid be a pollywog?
How can a twirl be a stream?
How can a bone be a book?
How can a sky be a star?
How can a rain be a cloud?
How can a flower be a scarf?

Group poems are based on the same process. In this case, the book *The Hungry Thing*, by Jan Slepian, had stimulated hungry monster play. The teacher asked the children to complete the sentence, "I'm so hungry I could eat . . . ," then took time to arrange the responses in a poetic form:

The Hungry Poem
By Shirley, Matt, Marina, and Tony, ages four to seven

I'm so hungry I could eat a peas pot
A lamp
A creek
A whole bottle of apple juice.
I'm so hungry I could eat a woodpecker
And a woodpecker's beak.
I'm so hungry I could eat two of the biggest alligators in the world.

I EAT PEOPLE

I'm so hungry I could eat a house
The top story
And the bottom story.

I EAT HOUSES

I'm so hungry I could eat a road
A road that goes everywhere.

I EAT DOGS AND TREES

I'm so hungry I could eat the world all in one gulp
The whole world
And the people and houses.

I would go to Pluto and eat Pluto.
I would go to the sun and eat the sun.
I would go to the coldest planet and take a little bit of it because
The sun is so hot
And the clouds are my drink.
I would suck all the water out of the clouds.
I would go to Santa Cruz and eat Santa Cruz.
I would go to Silver Spring and eat Silver Spring.
I'm so hungry I could eat a coffeepot
On a ketchup plate.
I'm so hungry I could eat a spoon of applesauce
That rains out
And floods all over the house.

Creating Books from Children's Stories

Once I see that children are able to make up full stories, with a beginning, middle, and end, I ask them if they want to make their own books. We look at picture books and books children had made in previous years and discuss the differences between text and illustration, author and artist. I either record their stories on a tape recorder, or write their stories as they dictate them. Then I write them out on separate pages, with room for illustrations. (Some children prefer to draw illustrations first, then tell a story about the pictures.) Older children can help decide which words go on which page. We staple them together, sew them together with yarn, or put them inside clear plastic binders. If a child is willing to leave her book at school, I read it at circle time, and keep it on the bookshelves with the other picture books. Children love to hear that they are authors and illustrators—one child had me make a large sign to pin on her shirt that said, "Author." It was so popular that more children wanted to create books just to get one.

Some years, when a particular play theme and story catches the imagination of a large group of children, I have been able to take the storytelling one step further, to create a group book. This process can take several months. Some children will maintain interest, while others will come and go. Usually, there are three or four children who are most interested in developing the story and bringing it to life through their play. This core group will provide the basic story. Then, over the course of several weeks, I ask small clusters of children, "Do you want to know what is happening in our story so far?" and I read to them, sometimes while they are playing the game. I occasionally read the developing story to the whole class at circle time. Each time I read it, I ask, "What else happens in this story?" As the story grows, I provide props that will help them play out their ideas.

When the story seems complete, I divide it into pages and post them on a bulletin board, where parents and staff can read it aloud. Children who are interested can choose pages to illustrate, in any art medium they would like. Sometimes, I'll devote an entire circle time to art, with everyone choosing a scene to draw. As children finish them, I post the illustrations next to the text, and work with the most motivated children to finish any that are not done.

When everything is ready, I mount the pages on posterboard and get it spiral bound to make an oversized book. Sometimes I'll include photos of the children's play that happened as we created the story. The book stays out in the book area for everyone to read. I have had children visit my classroom years later and ask to see the book they helped make.

For more information about bringing writing and storytelling into the classroom, read

Bloom, Carol Ann. *Playing with Print: Fostering Emergent Literacy.* Santa Monica, CA: Goodyear Publishing, 1997.

Dyson, Anne Haas. *Writing Superheroes: Contemporary Childhood, Popular Culture, and Classroom Literacy.* New York: Teachers College Press, 1997.

Paley, Vivian Gussin. *The Boy Who Would Be a Helicopter: The Uses of Storytelling in the Classroom.* Cambridge: Harvard University Press, 1990.

Using Dolls, Puppets, and Flannelboard Characters

Another way I introduce new superhero story lines to my class is to involve my dolls, puppets, and flannelboard characters. I have already shared several stories of how I integrate them into the classroom, helping them come alive by treating them as a member of the group and giving each a history, unique interests, and a family. I use them at circle times to help me create new stories, starting with tales based on the everyday happenings in children's lives. I ask a basic question, and the children come up with problems and think through solutions. What should Jalen have for breakfast today, and who will cook it? What can Rosie do if Mickie falls off his bike and hurts his knee? Will Harvey get angry if Kima takes his new kitten away? Sometimes I have the children play out the answers as we make them up. As the children get used to this process, the problems become more fantastic. How can we get food to Saul, who is pretending to be a shivering bear who can't sleep? How can Emily dive under the ocean to fix a hole in the earth? How can you rescue Zora if she is stuck on the moon? I look for ideas that combine the children's play scenarios with the curriculum interests of my staff.

My pretend children are also handy when the group can't seem to come to a consensus about where a story should go. If they can't decide, I tell them that one of the dolls or puppets will choose, and I bring a character out to tell them how the story will proceed. The class rarely questions the decision. I've had children stand up at circle and say knowingly, "You're really talking for that doll, aren't you." I tell them the truth— that I am pretending the doll is talking, and that storytelling often involves pretending. When I first started using dolls as members of my classroom, I thought this would destroy the fun for everyone. It has never happened. The child usually repeats the question for two or three days, but never stops believing that the dolls are alive. A month later, some other child will suddenly stand up and say, "You're talking for that puppet, aren't you?" Each child seems to need to discover this fact on their own, but they never let go of the fun and mystery of making an inanimate object come alive.

When I am telling stories through dolls and puppets, I use the children's words, but I have a lot of control over which ideas we will include and how problems will be solved. If children are proposing a story line that involves violence, for example, I don't reject it out of hand. I ask the other children if they approve of the idea. One child, who suggested that a boy doll should kill all the girls as part of a story, was shocked when I asked the girls in the room if they wanted to participate, and they all said clearly and firmly, "No!" At other times, I will have the characters play out the ideas to show the consequences. For example, a child suggested that Jalen punch Mickie to stop him from taking his blocks. I pretended Jalen got very angry and belligerent, and he punched Mickie on the arm. Mickie cried, but so did Jalen—he hurt his hand! He complained that when he saw people punching on the TV, it didn't look like it hurt, but the children agreed that the TV was wrong. I asked Jalen if he still wanted to solve the problem that way, and he said no, so the children came up with less violent alternatives.

An important element in making these stories succeed is providing props that children can then use to re-create and extend the stories later through their own play. Imagined tales told at circle time are fun, but children think best with their bodies, and they need to play out their own ideas if they are to develop them further. So if Harvey, the puppet, puts his miniature doll, Angie, into a car seat and drives her to the doctor, we will try to bring in a car seat and set up a car and a doctor's office. While it can sometimes be a scramble to come up with play materials when children take a story in an unexpected direction, to me it's part of the fun of teaching.

Here is an example of a rescue story that a four-year-old group wrote and later illustrated. It started from one child's interest in Rescue Rangers, and used a puppet named Sad Dog and his stuffed animal friend, Diamond Gold:

Sad Dog and the Very Very Very Hot Lava that Was Very Very Very Very Deep

One day, Sad Dog flew and bumped his head and fell into a hot lava swimming pool that was very, very, very hot and very, very, very, very deep.

He said, "I can swim in the hot lava, but I'm trying to trick all the people." So he tried to save himself by climbing up a tree, but it was too hard for him.

Then he wasn't so happy. It was hot, so hot, and he hurt himself and his eyeballs.

He asked Diamond Gold the Frog to rescue him, but he was in so deep that the frog couldn't swim. "Help," cried Sad Dog. "Rescue me! Please, rescue me before I die."

Then the Rescue Heroines and Heroes heard him calling, "Help! Help!"

They got their grappling hook and said, "Shalabala!" and pushed the button. It picked Sad Dog up by his ears and took him to Rocky Canyon.

Sad Dog said, "Gracias!" On the mountain, he walked to school and crawled into his rainbow bag.

Meanwhile, Diamond Gold was still in the hot lava, but the Rescue Heroines and Heroes said, "Shalabaloo!" and saved him with their capes.

They flew away with the frog to find Sad Dog at school.

They were so happy to be friends and safe. They had circle time and played games, but they never sat, and they never went to snack or anyplace because they were not hungry and they were too happy.

The End

For other views on using dolls for storytelling, see

Brown, Babette. *Combating Discrimination: Persona Dolls in Action.* Stone on Trent, UK: Trentham Books, 2001.

Whitney, Trisha. *Kids Like Us: Using Persona Dolls in the Classroom.* St. Paul: Redleaf Press, 1999.

Creating Theater from Children's Play

Creating books is not the only way to help children tell their superhero stories. Some teachers love to put on theater productions based on picture books or the children's own ideas. These can be done either with children taking part in the story or with puppets. Staging plays with preschool-age children takes great care. It's easy to get hooked on a script that uses children as mouthpieces for adult words. Watching a preschool play is painful when children stand stiffly and stare at the ceiling in panic while trying to remember a script that makes little sense to them. That takes away much of the potential for the children to be creative.

Saundra, a family child care provider, uses a more age-appropriate method for putting on productions with the twelve children in her care. Every year, she creates a new play based on the children's and staff's interests, with a role for anyone who wants to participate. She uses it to create a sense of community among the children, staff, and families. Her goal is to put on a production that combines music, art, craft, and storytelling without relying on assigned characters or lines that have to be memorized. She prefers plays where children can create their own roles and words and could change them up to the last minute. She also incorporates the talents of parents and other family members whenever she can. Here is how she created one of her plays, called "The Dreamseekers."

The children in Saundra's school were discussing their Halloween costumes, and several had plans to be superheroes. These were the same four- and five-year-olds with active imaginations and lots of fears. They loved to play war games that often became unsafe. That year, they had an added ingredient to cope with—the aftermath of the attack on the World Trade Center in New York. Their talk often focused on nightmares. While the youngest children didn't remember their dreams, the older ones had clear memories of monsters and disasters in their sleep.

Saundra started her process by noticing her children's interest in nightmares and writing down their words:

I was in this haunted house. I heard three different sounds and there were these big monsters and they were scary. I saw this big thing swinging from the wall, and it landed on its feet. And then I saw him, a different Spider-Man. It shot webs out of its stomach.
—Robert, age four

There were guns in my nightmare. The guns without names. They were pretends. There were swords in my nightmare. And there were masks, scary masks. What could make me safe? —Grant, age four

---

My monster came after me. I was chasing him and she got up and then I chased her again and she went outside and I got my tennis shoes on and shot her and shot her, and I chased her again and again and again the whole second! And then I woke up and my monster kicked me out of bed, and me and my monster started to fight! —Bettina, age five

---

I was riding on top of a earthquake. I was lying on a bed on the earthquake. —Rena, age three

Saundra's staff tried a variety of curriculum topics that they hoped would help the children face their fears and become powerful as a group without hurting one another. They brought information about trains, spiders, clouds, cats, and eagles into the school as the children showed interest in them. The children enjoyed each of these topics, but none of them sparked the kind of group play that Saundra was looking for.

Saundra also had several families that wanted her to explore their Native American backgrounds with the children. They helped her select picture books that featured stories from a variety of tribes. The book, *Buffalo Hunt*, by Donald Swainson, was the one that first grabbed her children's interest and led to the curriculum that changed their play. A few children started playing buffalo hunt games, and the game spread until almost all the children were participating. The teachers and families helped them set up a village and a fire pit. They visited local Native American sites and held a family feast. The children became more attentive to stories from native cultures.

Saundra found that many of the legends she was reading featured animals working together to overcome fear and solve a problem. As the children's play grew, Saundra saw an opportunity to create a new story, one that captured her children's imaginations, stimulated their creativity, and helped them think about their fears. When it came time to choose a theme for the year's production, she drew inspiration from several of the strands that were happening in the school: the children's focus on monsters and nightmares; the trickster character, Coyote, who appeared in many of the Native American legends they were reading; and the book, *Raven: A Trickster Tale from the Pacific Northwest,* by Gerald McDermott, about a raven who transformed into a child to bring the sun's light to humans in the dark days of winter.

Saundra and her staff decided to make Coyote the character in the play who needed help, and to give the children heroic roles. The idea they worked out with the children was that Coyote couldn't sleep because a monster had stolen his dreams, so he needed superheroes to travel into the night world to retrieve them. But who was the stealer of dreams? What powers would the children use to rescue them?

They realized that the Dream Stealer role was central to the success of the play. Some of the children envisioned a monster they could trick or defeat in battle. Others had ideas for a character who would help them in their quest to find the lost dreams. The staff helped them make lists of their nightmares and dream helpers, hoping that one clear idea would emerge, but none did. The lists helped Saundra see that the Dream Stealer needed to have two faces—one a nightmare, the other a helper—so that each child could choose the one they wanted. The Dream Stealer became a character that could transform from good guy to bad guy.

The idea of transformation became central to the play. Saundra decided to see if children could create characters for themselves that changed, as well, with one personality for the day world and a more powerful personality for traveling into the night world and retrieving Coyote's dreams. Some of the older children were able to understand her idea, and they helped the younger children plan their characters.

Amanda, one of Saundra's assistants, worked with the children to help them create costumes for the roles they selected. She designed a simple, reversible cape for them to decorate, so they could easily transform from their day character to their night character and back again. She asked the children to draw pictures of their characters, which she used as guides for making their costumes. She helped each one decide what magic powers they possessed and how they would use their powers to get Coyote's dreams back. The staff asked family members to help their children write down dreams that

(continued on page 131)

Here is the list of nightmares and dream helpers Saundra's class came up with while they planned their play:

The Nightmares

Monsters are really tall, bigger than my bedroom. They are normally black but they can turn into a disappearing clear. —*Stephan, age four*

There's a monster trap that looks like a road map. The monsters think it's bread and butter and a sandwich, but there's dynamite in it and he bites it and, whoa! Boom! —*Grant, age four*

Bears. One big, one little. A baby and a mom or dad. — *Nidya, age three*

Robbers who talk mean. — *Mallory, age five*

The FBI guys. They're actually robbers. They wear all black clothes and are about a hundred pounds. —*Robert, age four*

Ghosts —*Bettina, age five*

Dream Helpers

Bunny helpers transform when they are in trouble or sad or hurt. They kind of have sparkles. They can make bad things turn into other things, and the magic will follow. —*Ellen, age four*

Lions. A sports lion plays baseball and cracks the ball open. An ice power lion can do anything with ice. A rock power lion can do anything with rocks. And a fire lion can burn anything! —*Rena, Darian, and Sarah, all age four*

A unicorn came to me. It was all white with white feathers and a rainbow horn. I rode it into the sky. The clouds were strong enough to walk on, they pushed together into a floor. The clouds turned into stairs so me and my unicorn could walk up the stairs. The clouds made a house for us to walk in. —*Mallory, age five*

There was once a snow leopard that was best friends with a cloud leopard. —*Tam, age four*

An eagle swooped down and I got scared, but then it licked me and said, "Hello." Then it followed me home and it was my old pet. —*Grant, age four*

Here are some of the children's ideas for their two-sided characters:

I'm a human in the awake world. Then I'm a rabbit trickster. Tricking is going to be my power. I'm going to take back bad dreams from monsters and stuff, so I can get rid of them. —*Stephan*

I'm Spider-Man and Tarzan. In the beginning, I'm Spider-Man, just because I like him more than Tarzan. Tarzan has friends—monkeys and apes. He just has underwear for his costume. He's just a plain old person. —*Darian*

I want to be a princess, then a bright queen. Princesses have shorter dresses, and queens have longer dresses. —*Rena*

I'll be Indiana Jones in the daytime and morning, and an old man at night. Indiana Jones has weapons and is a rescuer, but the old man would find the dreams to take back to Indiana Jones. He would climb over six deserts, one hundred mountains, and then he would find them. He would load up the dreams in a big backpack. —*Robert*

I'm a flower, because flowers are beautiful. A blue flower, then a pink one. I love colors. I like to smell the colors, so I'll be a flower both times. I'll keep the dreams inside my head while I smell the flowers. —*Ellen*

I'm a pom-pom tummy. It has spots on it. There's two costumes, one an eyeball and one a pom-pom tummy. I'll be a baseball player, then a pom-pom tummy. —*Grant*

I'm a person. Then I put on my ninja costume and then I scare them and then I run away. —*Tam*

A house cat, and then a wild cat. They scratch! —*Bettina*

A kitty, then a pussy willow. —*Sarah*

A rainbow, then an owl. —*Nidya*

An ocean, then a leopard. —*Sauren*

A unicorn with wings, both times. —*Mallory*

they wanted to rescue and bring to Coyote, and they made a dream pillow with dream words attached for each child.

Amanda also created costumes for the two adult characters: a two-sided monster/ helper hat for the Dream Stealer, and a simple fur for Coyote. Several older brothers and sisters who had graduated from Saundra's school asked if they could participate, as well, so they helped Amanda with costumes and helped create the rest of the stage props.

In the meantime, Saundra worked with parents to paint a day sky on half of the garage door and a night sky on the other half. They put wheels on an old boat and painted it gold to transport children from the day world to the night world. They attached a basket to a pulley to keep the Dream Pillows slightly out of reach. They recorded music to play while the children rowed from one world to another, and rewrote the song, "Moon Shadow" by Cat Stevens, into a Dreamseeker theme. They wrote the words on large paper, so everyone could sing along.

There were no set lines in the play. Children could explain their characters and their magic powers to the audience, if they wanted to. They got to choose how they would engage the Dream Stealer and how they would escape. They practiced their roles during the week before the play, often changing what they did each time. Saundra rehearsed the whole production with the children only once, on the morning of the play.

The evening of the play, everyone brought potluck food to share. The families sat in the front yard on blankets, hay bales, car hoods, and folding chairs to watch the play. Neighbors were invited to join the crowd.

Coyote lay awake on a blanket, tossing and turning. The Dream Stealer waited in the night world, guarding the basket of dreams she had taken from Coyote. A parent played the Dreamseeker theme as everyone sang along:

> I'm calling out for the Dreamseekers
> Dreamseekers, Dreamseekers
> Calling for help from those Dreamseekers
> Dreamseekers, Dreamseekers
>
> Poor Coyote's lost her spark
> She's so frightened of the dark
> Poor Coyote's lost her spark
> Oh yi-i-i-i-ip, yi-i-i-ip
> Oh yi-i-i-ip, AIYEEEEE

Saundra called two children to the front for the next verse:

> She needs Grant and Bettina's aid
> Then she won't be so afraid
> She needs Grant and Bettina's aid
> Oh yi-i-i-i-ip, yi-i-i-ip
> Oh yi-i-i-ip, AIYEEEEE

Grant was dressed as a baseball player, Bettina as a cat. Saundra helped them describe their characters and how they would transform to get Coyote's dreams back. Then they climbed into the boat and started rowing. Parent volunteers pushed and wiggled the wheeled boat from the day side to the night. The children got out and transformed into their night world self by turning their capes inside out. Grant became a Pom-Pom Tummy, with colored Ping-Pong balls attached to his costume with Velcro. He distracted the roaring Dream Stealer monster by throwing the balls, then climbed on a small ladder to grab one of the Dream Pillows. Sarah turned into a wild cat who showed her claws to convince the Dream Stealer to help her climb the ladder. Once they both had Dream Pillows for Coyote, they jumped into the boat, returned to the day world, and transformed back into their day characters. They put the Dream Pillows into Coyote's Dream Bag, then waited to see if Coyote could fall asleep. She could not; she still rolled on her bed and cried.

Another group of children was called to make the journey, then another and another. Some found a monster who roared and resisted their attempts to grab a Dream Pillow; others found a helper who showed them the way. Some climbed the ladder; some asked their parents to help them fly up to the Dream Basket. In the end, everyone brought a dream back to Coyote's Dream Bag, until Coyote had recovered all her dreams. She thanked them all, and fell blissfully asleep as everyone sang her a lullaby.

A parent had secretly tied all the Dream Pillows together in a long line with multi-colored strings. Saundra magically pulled them out of the Dream Bag as everyone sang. Party treats for every child were attached to the end of the line.

Saundra's work with dramatics shows another way that teachers can take issues and ideas that are important to children, combine them with the skills and interests of the staff, and use them to touch on all other aspects of the curriculum and appeal to almost all the children in a group.

Here are some of the stories Saundra and her staff read to children while creating the Dreamseekers play:

Baylor, Byrd. *Coyote Cry.* New York: Lothrop, Lee & Shepard, 1972.

Bierhorst, John. *The People with Five Fingers: A Native Californian Creation Tale.* Tarrytown, NY: Marshall Cavendish, 2000.

Doner, Kim. *Buffalo Dreams.* Portland, OR: WestWinds Press, 1999.

Goble, Paul. *Dream Wolf.* New York: Bradbury Press, 1990.

Grimm, Jakob, and Wilhelm Grimm, retold by Jane Werner. *The Twelve Dancing Princesses.* New York: Simon and Schuster, 1954.

Hobbs, Will. *Beardream.* New York: Atheneum, 1997.

Keams, Geri. *Grandmother Spider Brings the Sun: A Cherokee Story.* Flagstaff, AZ: Northland, 1995.

London, Jonathan. *Fire Race: A Karuk Coyote Tale.* San Francisco: Chronicle Books, 1993.

McDermott, Gerald. *Raven: A Trickster Tale from the Pacific Northwest.* San Diego: Harcourt, 1993.

Oughton, Jerrie. *How the Stars Fell into the Sky: A Navajo Legend.* Boston: Houghton Mifflin, 1992.

Steptoe, John. *The Story of Jumping Mouse.* New York: Lothrop, Lee & Shepard, 1984.

Swainson, Donald. *Buffalo Hunt.* Olympic Marketing Corporation, 1980.

Taylor, Harriet Peck. *Coyote Places the Stars.* New York: Simon and Schuster, 1993.

Transforming Media Characters into New Stories

Many children rely on media characters and story lines for their play stories because they provide an easy way to keep a group game going. These stories often use bad guy or monster characters to represent the plot problem, and good guys with big guns to defeat them. While I will write down these stories when individual children want me to, I avoid using them in group stories. However, some preschoolers refuse to veer too far from the TV and movie scripts they have seen, or accept anything but commercially made props based on their favorite characters, and they get upset when other children try to change the game. The resulting stories and the play that is based on them can be frustrating for parents and teachers—repetitive, violent, and unimaginative. It rarely works to force these children to give up their vision of what their play should look like. Adult explanations and lectures on this subject won't convince children to change their taste in superheroes. So how can teachers help children move past these media-based stories to create new ones?

I try to accept whatever images come through my door inside children's minds, even if I wish they weren't there. I won't promote them by buying related toys, books, or posters or making them a focus of my curriculum plans, but I don't attack them either. I find it more helpful to inquire about them with questions that can broaden children's ideas of who their characters are and what they can do. I focus on helping children imagine the life their character might have when he or she is not on duty. Even super-heroes have to eat and sleep sometime! And even bad guys and monsters can have feelings and care about friends and family.

Here are some examples of questions that have had a positive effect on play:

★ I wonder what kind of pets Superman and Superwoman have? I wonder what they named them? What do they do when their pets are sick? According to my class, Supermen and -women are partial to wolves and bears. These questions brought a group of Superfolk into the veterinary hospital play we had set up, and led to an interest in learning about animal record-holders—which animal is the fastest, strongest, biggest, and so on.

★ Do Ninja Turtles sleep with stuffed animals? What kinds? Do they use blankets? What colors are their blankets? These resulted in a class chart of bedtime animals and blanket colors.

★ Did Megaman use a bottle when he was a baby? How does Megaman take care of his own babies? My group of Megamen ended up carrying "megadolls" in "megabackpacks," with regular "megafeeding" breaks. It was really very sweet, but the "megapoop" talk got tiresome.

★ If you had a baby Pokemon, what would you call it? This led to children making up their own Pokemon cards and reducing their requests to parents for commer-cially made ones.

★ What kinds of foods do Powerpuff Girls eat? Where do they buy it? How do they cook their meals? (Within a few days of making a list based on these questions, we opened the Power Foods Restaurant in the sandbox.)

★ What do you think the wrestlers on TV read to their children at bedtime? My puppet, Harvey, wore a wrestling outfit (his wrestling name was Horrible Harvey) to circle one day and read a story to his toy hedgehog, Scrub Brush. A few of the wrestlers in my room were willing to read books to dolls, but I never did get them to write letters to the real wrestler/actors to ask that question. Oh, well.

When I'm talking to young children about commercial superheroes, I try to ask questions that will make these two-dimensional characters into more complex, realistic people, tie the superhero play into other curriculum themes going on in the room, and gradually move the stories away from the commercial characters.

Children may not respond to these kinds of questions at first. They may, in fact, think you're crazy. Be patient, and keep asking new ones. Sometimes children incorporate the answers into their play several days later.

Teacher: I wonder what kind of birthday present Superman would give to his best friend?

Superman, age three: What do you mean? Superman doesn't have any friends.

Superman, at the art table three days later: Teacher, I'm making a walkie-talkie that calls anyplace on Earth for Superman's friend. It's his birthday. Do you have any buttons?

For children who absolutely refuse to follow me down this path, I've had good luck asking them to make lists of superpowers their characters have and do not have. Then we make up a superhero that possesses some of the missing superpowers. We've created props and stories for the character, and once we acted out an entire show inside a large cardboard box with a "TV screen" cut out of it.

Media villains can also be transformed by helping children understand what might have motivated them to behave badly and finding humane ways to change them. This strategy has its limits; many children won't be satisfied with a superhero story unless bad guys die. Still, while tales full of death and destruction may temporarily satisfy children's need to defeat their fears, listening to too many of them can create even more fears. Even though children resist at first, I have found they will accept stories that don't depend on killing evil monsters with lethal weapons when there is an exciting story available that uses bravery and clever thinking to solve the problem. In the long run, such stories of transformation are more deeply rewarding for children than most of the ones featured on the TV screen, because they give real clues about how to be powerful in the real world.

STORIES FROM THE CLASSROOM

The Forgetting Monster's Treasure

Here's an example of how my staff worked with a child obsessed with a movie character, and transformed his monsters into a character the whole class could use for their play:

"Power Rangers! I'm the Blue, you're the Green, right? We're gonna kill that monster, right?"

That's how every school day started after four-year-old Enjay saw the Power Rangers movie. His preoccupation with the show became the focus of play for many of the three- and four-year-olds in my classroom. To the dismay of the teachers, the games he inspired were full of fear, anger, and violence. "Why can't they play a nicer game?" one of my aides asked. While I disliked the show and the aggressive play it often created, I knew that banning Power Rangers wouldn't help the children learn about friendship and power. I wanted to transform the play into something more cooperative and imaginative.

Power Rangers play was not new in my classroom — the TV series had been popular for several years. Enjay's older brother, Otan, had been a fan when I was his teacher, so I knew that Enjay had been watching the show since infancy. It was, in fact, a morning ritual that helped bond the five children in his family — boys and girls, toddlers and teenagers — and got them started on their day.

The energy behind Enjay's play increased dramatically, though, after seeing the movie. The experience of sitting in a crowded theater and watching his idols on the big screen had been overwhelming. He refused to believe that these new characters were the same as the ones on TV. "They were bigger," he said. "Their guns were more bigger too. And they had bigger magic in them."

Before the movie, Enjay was able to step in and out of his Blue Ranger role. He could take on vast powers on the playground, then become four-year-old Enjay again during circle time, art projects, lunch, and nap. He could follow the safety rules and talk about conflicts. He could be a play leader for superhero games, then follow other people's orders when he participated in house and puppy dog games.

Once the movie introduced the new, larger-than-life Power Rangers to him, though, the Enjay we knew rarely appeared. He seemed to have been taken over by an alien force, one that was loud, competitive, and often unsafe. He let us know that Blue Power Rangers never do art or nap or circle. They don't let anybody else take turns, they can't be bothered with walking inside or sitting down for a meal, and they certainly never pretend to be babies or puppies.

Enjay's obsession quickly conquered the classroom. Five boys and two girls (both Pink Power Rangers) became part of his inner circle. Another group of children became anti–Power Rangers and bonded by worrying and complaining about the play. Some of them were genuinely afraid; others seemed fascinated and wanted to join in, but were unable to let themselves participate, except as an occasional whining victim.

The play consisted of four main actions: running, morphing (also called "murphing" or "transmorphing"), arguing, and killing. After putting on colored capes, the children would run around on the climbing structure, or circle the yard. They argued as they ran:

"I'm transmorphing into a rocket. Zoom!"

"*No.* Yellow Rangers can't be rockets, they're tigers."

"*No.* I'm the Cheetah Power Ranger."

"That's so stupid. Power Rangers can't morph to cheetahs."

"So? Now I'm a rocket car and I'm faster than you."

While these discussions were a constant part of the play, if they in any way challenged Enjay's position as leader, we knew we had to stand close by, because a fistfight was imminent.

All the running and transforming and arguing were unimportant, though, compared to the main event: killing the monster. At first, Enjay tried to assign the role of monster to another child, but the Rangers were so ferocious in their attacks that no one wanted the job. So the monster became an imaginary beast that would attack, imprison, and eat children at Enjay's command. Everyone watched Enjay to know what horrible things the monster was doing and to whom, what weapons would be effective against it, and when exactly the monster lived and died. On days when Enjay was absent, the game often fell apart, with several not-so-powerful Rangers drifting about, wondering, "What would Enjay do?"

The story details varied from day to day. The monster lived in a tree, in a cave, in the river, under a rock. It ate children, stole money, poisoned puppies, or chased mommies out of town. It had sharp teeth, claws that could shoot fire, wings, yellow fur, and eyes that killed. It had three eyes, one eye, a million eyes, or no eyes at all. It could only die if you stabbed it, shot it, burned it, cut its head off, or drowned it in acid hot lava.

The monster had three feelings: hunger, anger, and hate.

A typical day found the monster sucking all the blood and air from people. It was mad because it had eaten poison. Two children had already died, and it was attacking a third when the Blue, Green, Black, and Pink Power Rangers chased it into a trap, surrounded it, and killed it with blaster guns. The monster came back to life several times, and wasn't dead for sure until Enjay pulled its eyes out.

After a few weeks, it was clear that this play was not a short-term distraction, but a serious game that would dominate the curriculum for quite some time. Parents were concerned about the scary tone and the gory subject matter. Staff reaction varied. Some wanted to create a few restrictions on where it could take place, while others wanted to ban it completely. Attempts to impose new safety regulations were largely unsuccessful and became more and more punitive. We tried distracting them with new science curriculum, a new veterinary hospital in the dramatic play area, and lots of opportunities for large motor art. Most of the children participated and loved the new activities, but the monster killing continued every day.

One day, during a break in the action, I asked Enjay, "Why is the monster so angry at the Power Rangers?"

"Because he's a bad guy monster. Bad guys are angry," Enjay answered in a gruff voice.

"Did something happen that made the monster so angry?"

Enjay thought for a few seconds, then replied in a voice that was closer to normal. "He's mad at the Power Rangers. They stole all his powers, but the witch tattletaled on them."

"I didn't think Power Rangers stole things."

"Only from bad guys. The bad guy monster stoled from people and killed them, so the Power Rangers stoled stuff back and killed the monster, and they won."

"What did the monster steal?"

"Some cool stuff. But he hided it," Enjay said, and he walked away.

Later in the day, Enjay stopped running long enough to tell me, "The monster stoled treasure. Gold and jewels. He hided it in a hole, and the Power Rangers are looking for it." After lunch, Enjay added a new element to his game — digging in the sand for lost treasure.

My questions were not designed to divert Enjay's attention or change his game. I was simply curious, but I had stumbled onto questions that had engaged Enjay's storytelling ability. It was the first time anything I did made a difference in the game.

The Rangers didn't find any treasure, though, so Enjay had them pretend to smash the monster with plastic shovels.

The next day, I asked the group, "Does your monster have a name?"

"No!" some of them replied immediately, including Enjay.

Others thought about it. "I think his name is Buster."

"No, it's Sourpuss."

"No, it's Sourgrass."

"That's stupid. His name is really Cave Man Killer."

"It sounds like the monster is a boy," I said.

"Sure," Enjay said, "because it's a bad guy monster. Girls can't be bad guys, only boys."

"I thought there was a woman on the Power Rangers TV show that's supposed to be a bad guy," I said.

"No," said Enjay, "she's a mean witch." Everyone agreed, even the children who had never watched the show before.

"Maybe we can choose a monster name at circle time," I said.

"At circle time?" They looked at each other, first with confusion, then with delight. "We can name the monster at circle time!"

I had acknowledged the importance of their game by allowing it into the official "work time" of the school. The news spread, and I had no trouble getting everyone to circle that day.

I have helped children name many things at my circles: dolls, puppets, stuffed animals, worms, and kittens. I once had a child ask me to help name her new baby sister, because she didn't like the name her parents had chosen. We had most recently named two toy hedgehogs Scrub Brush and Smoothie for my puppet Harvey. I use several strategies when picking names with a group. I first make a list of everybody's ideas, one per child. No name is excluded unless it is insulting, profane, or the name of someone already in the class. Sometimes, there is a clear favorite, and the decision is made. Usually, I read back the list and put off the decision until the next day. Then I try to get a sense of the favorites by talking to children individually. I sometimes edit out the ones I can't stand — there's always a child who wants to call everything Rainbow Princess Delight, and I'm sorry, but I just can't live with that. The next day, I announce the two or three favorites and take a vote. Since preschoolers don't understand the concept of "one person, one vote," everybody can vote as many times as they want. The name with the most votes wins. Sometimes, the children create a compromise by combining two of the names. That's how my stuffed cat got the name Xeena Dress. If nothing else works, I tell the children that my puppet, Sad Dog, will make the decision. He always seems to choose the one I like best, but the children rarely argue with Sad Dog.

None of these routines worked on the monster. It was Enjay's monster, and everybody knew it. He insisted that it had no name, not even No Name, a suggestion from Marta (the Pink Power Ranger) that I thought was brilliant.

"Then I'll name my own monster," one child said, "and I'll call him whatever I want. I'll call him Boo Goo Goo."

Suddenly, I had seventeen children calling out names, or arguing for no names at all. This was not what I had in mind as a community-building exercise. "Time to eat," I called, but the arguments went right through hand washing, snack time, and beyond. I had aroused their passion, but I wasn't sure what to do with it.

Children came up to me the rest of the day, telling me names. I wrote them down, but I didn't make any promises:

> Mr. No Eyes
> Big Guy
> Shallabanger
> Cookie Monster
> Super Power Monster
> Super Power Super Man Monster
> Super Power Super Man Monster in the River of Doom
> Cry Baby
> Hot Lava Monster with Hot Lava in His Throat
> The Creep
> Stinger Bee (this child had been stung by a yellow jacket the day
>   before)
> Bad Billy Gruff Ghost
> Bad Candy Monster

No one agreed with anyone else's name. Everybody had their own, personal vision of the creature they had been killing for weeks. I didn't know what to do until a child showed me a drawing.

"Here's mine," she said.

"Your drawing?" I asked.

"My monster," she said. "Write on it—'This is the Big Guy.'"

The next day at circle, I brought lots of pens and paper. I announced that, instead of our usual group time activities, we would have a drawing circle. Anyone could draw a monster and give it a name. The teachers would write down any words children dictated, then we would hang the pictures on the wall.

Every child drew at least one. Some drew four or five, continuing right through snack time. By the time they were done, we had covered an 8 by 4-foot section of wall with monsters of all kinds, from an abstract, single-color scribble with no name at all to a monster with multicolored toes, wings, tongues, teeth, and three eyes, named Three Eyes Bat. Enjay's was called Power Ranger Bad Guy Monster, and he had spent a lot of time drawing teeth and claws.

After snack I started reading from the pictures on what became known as the "Monster Wall," and almost every child came by to listen. There was no arguing, not even from Enjay. The children sat or stood quietly, occasionally making comments about the coolness or scariness of a particular drawing. The children were amazed to discover that everyone had their own vision of what a scary monster looks like.

Then we came to Nicholas' drawing. Nicholas, one of the youngest children in the group but one of the most skilled with words, had drawn an amorphous green blob and colored the inside purple. There was nothing unusual about it, except the name: the Forgetting Monster. The children recognized that this was a strange name for a monster — not scary or angry, but silly, even sad. They asked Nicholas what his monster forgot.

"He's sad because he forgot where he buried his treasure. And because he forgot his name."

Two of the five-year-olds in the group thought that was the funniest joke they had ever heard. "He forgot his name, and his name was the Forgetting Monster?" They repeated the joke at least five times, each time falling on the floor on top of each other. Enjay and some of the four-year-olds joined the activity, laughing hysterically, even though they didn't have a clue why it was funny. Nicholas was baffled. "It's not funny," he pleaded quietly. "He really forgot."

After that, everyone called the monster in the Power Rangers game the Forgetting Monster. Fewer and fewer children were willing to kill it, because they knew its sad story. The focus of the play shifted, and the children spent hours helping the monster search for his lost treasure. Enjay resisted at first, but he turned out to be one of the Forgetting Monster's biggest helpers, and seemed relieved to have a monster around that was not so terrifying.

The staff supported this play with treasure hunts, a Forgetting Monster cave, Forgetting Monster memory games, heroine and hero medals, and more drawing at circle time. As the play developed, I kept asking questions:

"What happens next?"

"What did he forget now?"

"How are they going to solve that problem?"

I wrote down the children's words on our dictation boards. We read through their words every few days, sometimes at circle, sometimes in small groups, and the children discussed what should be included in the story. I had children choose two of our classroom dolls, Jalen and Rosie, to be characters in the story. A dragon and a giant joined the tale, along with surfing props from another fantasy play theme. A group of six children became the main authors, although almost everyone in the classroom contributed. The children often gave Enjay and Nicholas the final word. In places where the children couldn't seem to make a decision, I used two or three ideas, either the ones the children liked the best, or the ones I thought sounded the best.

After a month, I typed the story in big print and posted it on the Monster Wall, which kept expanding for many months. I asked children if they wanted to create illustrations, and eight children immediately took up the task. After half the illustrations were done, I mounted the pages and pictures on colored cardboard and added a spiral binding. The final illustrations took a few more weeks to finish.

In the end, about three months after Enjay saw the Power Rangers movie, our book was ready. It stayed in the book corner for the rest of the year, and children added their own storybooks to the collection. The final story, "The Forgetting Monster's Treasure," has no trace of Power Rangers or guns left in it. The children still pretended to be Power Rangers, but the game was much more organized and less violent, and the stories they acted out were their own, not imitations of the ones they had seen on the screen. One child's violent obsession had been transformed into a community-building group story.

Here is the story that emerged out of Enjay's Power Rangers play. It is the longest and most complex I have done with children:

The Forgetting Monster's Treasure

Rosie said, "What should we do today?"

Jalen said, "Let's go into the Heroines and Heroes Cave."

They both shouted, "Hooray!" and they ran to the Heroines and Heroes Cave.

Rosie and Jalen crawled in to the dark, dark cave. They heard someone call, "Help! Help!"

"What's that?" said Jalen. "Is it a shark tooth?"

"Is it a triceratops?" said Rosie.

"Is it a dragon?" said Jalen.

Then they heard, "Aaarrrhhhh . . . Go away!" It was a monster with eyes and a mouth, but no teeth. The monster was crying.

"Why are you crying?" said Jalen.

"I forgot where I buried my treasure," said the monster. "I need some friends to help me find it."

"We can help you," said Rosie. "We're heroines and heroes. What's your name?"

"I forgot," said the monster. "Maybe it's Sharktooth Sharkie. Maybe it's Gak. Maybe it's Quacky."

"We'll just call you the Forgetting Monster," said Jalen. "What kind of treasure did you lose?"

"I forgot," said the Forgetting Monster. "Maybe it's shark gold. Maybe it's tiger teeth. Maybe it's a magic crystal in a magic box."

"Where did you leave it?" said Rosie.

"I forgot," said the Forgetting Monster. "Maybe it splashed into the ocean. Maybe it's buried underground. Maybe a giraffe ate it. We should ask Belafar the Dragon. She'll remember."

"Where does she live?" said Jalen.

"I forgot," said the Forgetting Monster. "Maybe she lives in a jungle. Maybe she lives in a cubby. Maybe she lives inside the ceiling."

Then the children heard someone say, "You silly monster. I live in the cave next door." It was Belafar the Dragon.

"Hello," said Rosie. "Do you know where to find the treasure?"

"Yes," said Belafar. "I was flying through the air with Forgetting Monster on my back. He forgot to hold on to his bag of jewels. He dropped it over the beach, and it disappeared in the sand."

Rosie, Jalen, Belafar, and the Forgetting Monster walked to the beach. They started digging for the treasure. First, they dug a big hole and looked inside it, but nothing was there. Then they dug a bigger hole and looked inside it, but nothing was there. Finally they dug and dug and dug, until the hole was bigger than a cheetah, bigger than a dinosaur, bigger than a volcano. They looked inside it and saw something shiny.

"It's my treasure!" said the Forgetting Monster.

"We'll get it for you," said Rosie and Jalen and Belafar, and they jumped into the hole.

They picked up the treasure and tried to climb out, but the hole was too big. "Help, help," they cried.

The Forgetting Monster reached into the hole to get them, but his arm wasn't long enough. Then he threw a golden rope into the hole, but the rope wasn't long enough. Then he put a ladder into the hole, but the ladder wasn't long enough.

A surfer came and put his surfboard in the hole. Rosie and Jalen tried to climb up the surfboard, but it was too slippery.

"What should I do?" asked the Forgetting Monster.

"Call the giant," said Belafar. "She's our neighbor."

"Help us, giant!" cried the Forgetting Monster.

Then they heard footsteps and crashing, and they saw the giant. "Save us, giant!" said Jalen and Rosie and Belafar.

The giant had long, long arms. She reached into the hole, and everyone grabbed the giant's fingers. She pulled Rosie, Jalen, and Belafar out of the hole.

"Hooray!" everyone shouted.

"You're a heroine," said Rosie to the giant.

"You should get a medal," said Jalen.

"Everyone should get a medal for helping to find my treasure," said the Forgetting Monster.

So everyone got a medal. The giant got a medal that was as big as an ambulance, as big as a fire truck, as big as a school on a rocket ship.

"Hooray for heroines and heroes!" they all shouted. Then they went to the Forgetting Monster's house for a snack. They could eat it, but really, it's just on the page.

The End

CHAPTER 6

Fostering Heroism

"I'm a superhero.

That's what we do."

—Callie, age six, to an adult
who thanked her for
helping carry groceries

WITHOUT ADULT GUIDANCE, superhero play can end up reinforcing all the negative ways children relate, harming their connections to other people. Helping others, as Callie did, is a much more satisfying way for children to fill their need for both power and relationship, especially when they work together in a group. When young children become real heroines and heroes, the growth in their self-esteem, sense of empowerment, and feeling of belonging to a community are priceless.

Teachers often use curriculum that highlights each child's special qualities to raise self-esteem. That can be useful, but unless children also appreciate their ties to the people around them, self-esteem becomes egotism. This confusion about the definition of self-esteem has resulted in studies that cast doubt on its value, such as the research that finds high self-esteem among criminals. Our job as teachers is to support every child's self-awareness, but to do it in ways that inspire pride in their families and cultures while creating an inclusive, cooperative community. Small acts of heroism can help make that happen.

The dramatic play and storytelling described in previous chapters is a good way to introduce the ideas of heroism, but for children to truly understand it, they have to move from fantasy play to real action. Teachers can empower their children in these ways:

★ Bringing real heroes and heroines into the classroom
★ Engaging children in helper roles
★ Helping children develop a sense of justice
★ Setting up an inclusive classroom
★ Planning anti-bias, environmental, and other community projects

Bringing Real Heroes and Heroines into the Classroom

Before we can help children be heroines and heroes, we have to know what a real hero does. The common view of heroism is that it involves helping others in the face of danger. I prefer to use a broader definition of bravery and heroism with young children, because they are not mature enough to make good judgments about safety. I celebrate any time children overcome their reluctance to take action and show compassion or work for justice.

Heroism in our culture is sometimes confused with fame. The media create celebrities and call them heroes to grab our attention and sell products. Athletes, musicians, actors, and other stars are held up as role models for children. Many of these people deserve praise, because they have worked hard to develop their talents. Some have used their fame to speak up for justice and to do good deeds. But the focus is usually on their carefully packaged public images, rather than on their real lives and values. Children learn that people gain power by having beauty, wealth, and attitude. Girls, in particular, learn that the way to gain status is to be "sexy." Teachers should not fall into this trap.

The best way to counteract these bewildering images is to bring actual heroines and heroes into the classroom. They don't have to be famous. Plenty of people in your community take care of others or fight injustice: medical and emergency workers, foster parents, the father who serves meals to the homeless, the sister who helps rescue abandoned animals, the playground aide who helps solve fights at the elementary school, the cook who is making food for the children down the hall. Invite them in to share their stories! Let them know that you want them to focus on how it feels to help people, and ask them to bring pictures or other items that children can hold, look at, and, if possible, use.

There are other heroes who may not be available to visit but whose stories can be told through news articles, books, pictures, and music. Some are well-known figures with days set aside for celebration, such as Martin Luther King Jr., Abraham Lincoln, and Cesar Chavez. Some require more extensive research. One teacher has used a "birthday of the month" approach, choosing one local hero and one public figure to talk about and celebrate each month. She borrows any books she can find about the people for a special shelf, creates a bulletin board about their lives and work, talks about them at group times throughout the month, and celebrates their birthdays. She tries to pick individuals or groups whose work is understandable and interesting to young children, and who represent the full diversity of people.

Engaging Children in Helper Roles

Children who learn about real heroes want the chance to be heroines and heroes themselves. They don't need big, brave deeds to get started. There are many opportunities for them in the everyday routines teachers use to take care of their classrooms. Helping to prepare food, serve meals, clean, set up nap, care for plants and animals, and keep classroom records gives children a feeling of ownership of their school. Many teachers create a chart of daily jobs that can be rotated among the children. By making permanent individual name strips that fit in pockets or attach to the job chart with felt or Velcro, daily chores become part of the classroom literacy curriculum.

These regular routines prepare children to help out when less predictable situations arise, ones that require emotional or physical first aid. A child slips and falls. A toy breaks. Someone is crying by the door. These are times when children have to overcome their hesitation and choose to act, even though they aren't required to help out.

Publishers are now printing biographical picture books for preschool and early elementary school-age children, and they are gradually including more diverse subjects. Here are some series to check out if you are looking for real heroes and heroines to talk about in your classroom. Each has up to thirty different biographies available:

Photo-Illustrated Biographies by Bridgestone Books, a division of Capstone Press
Picture Book Biographies by Holiday House
First Biographies by Abdo and Daughters

You can also get background information on a variety of heroes and heroines on the Internet:

www.myhero.com—information on heroes in many different endeavors
www.wagingpeace.org—people who have worked for peace
www.womeninworldhistory.com—heroines throughout history
www.distinguishedwomen.com—biographies of heroines throughout history and links to related sites
www.greatwomen.org—Web site of the National Women's Hall of Fame in Seneca Falls, New York
www.blackseek.com/bh/—*Black History Daily* celebrates Black History month all year
www.africanamericans.com—African American history and culture
www.fau.edu/library/brodytoc.htm—Jewish American history and culture
www.gayheroes.com—gay and lesbian history and culture
www.nobel.se—Nobel laureates in physics, chemistry, medicine, literature, peace, and economics
www.booksense.com and www.amazon.com—find biographies by entering name in search box (limit your search to children's books)

That's one of the hallmarks of bravery. At first, children will need help making that choice, because they won't have a vision of what to do. They will stand close to a hurt or upset friend with looks of fear and worry on their faces. Some children will run away. Some will even get angry, because the other child's pain calls up similar feelings in themselves, and they don't like it. They want to do something, but they are waiting for guidance. This is especially true when the onlookers feel guilty because they had something to do with the injury, accidentally or not.

It doesn't take much effort to get them to help. They need permission to act and they need the proper tools nearby. When a child is crying because he misses his parent, children can comfort him by holding his hand, singing, or reading to him. When a book tears or the climbing structure has splinters, children can learn to respond appropriately if you make the proper tools available. When someone is injured, children can provide basic first aid with ice, washcloths, bandages, or a comfort toy.

Lunch box "emergency kits" that contain the materials children need to help with common mishaps make it easier for children to react. Store them where children can reach them and label them with pictures. Some examples:

- ★ A repair kit, decorated with pictures of tools and containing simple woodworking tools, such as sandpaper, a hammer, pliers, and a screwdriver

- ★ A first aid kit, with a red cross on it, holding bandages, a packet of wet wipes, a packet of tissues, small-size disposable gloves, a plastic bag, and a stethoscope. Teachers can add an ice pack or cold "rice baby" (a sock filled with rice and tied off at the end) from the freezer when needed. Let a child carry the kit in a backpack on walks and field trips. (Be sure that children do not have contact with another person's blood when they are helping with physical injuries.)

- ★ A clean-up kit, with a small towel, several sponges, a small broom and dustpan, and a plastic bag for trash

- ★ A book-doctor kit, with scissors and rolls of book-repair tape

Children will need clear rules about when these kits can be used. They shouldn't be used for play (although I have allowed children to use them when my classroom dolls have gotten "hurt"). Children should always ask the person who is hurt, "Do you want me to help?" You may have to establish a turn-taking system so the desire to lend a hand doesn't become a fistfight. Once the routines are established in your classroom, the response will become a habit—when someone is hurt or something is damaged, it's okay to help. The children who participate won't need a lot of praise to feel good about themselves, just a simple statement of thanks and recognition that they chose to act.

Helping Children Develop a Sense of Justice

Daily care routines help build compassion and empathy. Children must also develop a sense of justice to be true heroines and heroes. With practice, they can learn to listen to other people's points of view, come up with compromises that take everyone's needs into account, and speak up when they believe something is unfair. As five-year-old Jenna said, "Fair is when everybody gets everything, but nobody gets everything they want. Unfair is when somebody gets left out."

Teachers can make fairness part of their classroom's everyday vocabulary by asking for children's views about justice and holding back their own preconceptions of what is fair and not fair. Many adults dismiss young children's thoughts on this subject because those ideas can be so self-centered and unrealistic, and because most adults assume they know the best way to solve every problem. Accepting children's ideas about how to solve problems fairly, even when they are impractical or silly, can give teachers great insight into what children are learning about the subject. Those impossible ideas may be the seeds for a solution that will make everyone involved feel proud. By modeling sympathetic listening skills, teachers can help children listen to each other and develop a more complex and mature definition of justice.

Teachers don't have to wait long for fairness to become an issue in the classroom. It comes up all the time when children play in groups. When they have a conflict, observe how they try to solve the problem. Many have a hard time imagining that other people can have different, valid perspectives. Some will feel justified in defending their positions through physical or emotional attacks. All the children involved in an argument may feel they have been treated unfairly. The way adults step in to help with these daily disputes has a huge effect on children's understanding of justice. If adults treat children in ways that feel arbitrary and unfair to them, the children will turn around and treat each other unfairly. If adults give children an active voice in solving their own problems, even if those solutions aren't very successful, the children will create a clearer picture for themselves of what justice means. The adult's role is to facilitate the discussion and keep it safe, rather than make all the decisions. While it's easiest in the short term for teachers to step in and solve everything, helping children resolve some of their own conflicts teaches them important lessons about listening, empathy, and respect. As with superhero play, the goal is to welcome children's emotion, thinking, and energy into the curriculum so it can be used as part of the teaching process.

Here are some other responses I received to the questions, "What is fair?" and "What is unfair?"

When you have a fight but everybody is happy at the end, that's fair. —*Marcia, age five*

When somebody hits you, that's not fair. —*Juan, age four*

Or knocks down your blocks. —*Martin, age three*

Don't steal my toys. If you do, you have to go to jail. —*Brad, age three*

One person doesn't get to be the boss all the time. I don't like that. —*Zoe, age four*

You have to make sure everybody knows not to be mean. —*Scott, age five*

Everybody should get to talk. —*Semara, age three*

Everybody gets to vote. —*Thomas, age four*

Everybody should get the same. Everybody should be equal. —*Ema, age five*

If somebody get too much, that's not fair. —*Rebecca, age four*

No bad words or names. No hitting or spitting. No guns. No bad guys. —*Kyle, age three*

But yes to puppies! —*Kristen, age four*

Clear conflict resolution routines that build children's sense of justice are an important part of any classroom. Here are several details to keep in mind:

★ Intervene immediately to stop a child who is being dangerous. Children can't solve problems when they are being hurt.

★ Don't assume children understand what the problem is. Clarify what is happening by stating what you observe without making judgments, and by giving the children involved a chance to tell you their views. "I see you holding the block in the air, and your friend is trying to reach it. You both look angry to me. Can you tell me what happened?"

★ Let children express their feelings. Adults tend to rush past feelings to try to resolve the problem, especially when children are communicating through tears, tantrums, or angry words. It's difficult for children to listen and think clearly when they are full of emotion and worried that they will not be heard. Take a few minutes to let feelings come out, so children can calm down and solve their own problems successfully. That doesn't mean adults have to give children whatever they want when they scream and cry; it means taking their feelings seriously and not shortchanging their need to discharge them.

★ Model good listening. Each child needs time to speak, which means others must be able to listen. That's not easy during stressful times, even for adults. Teachers should demonstrate how to pay attention to another person's ideas without dismissing them, and how to reflect back what they have heard.

★ Focus on the children's underlying goals rather than their mistakes. Even when a child's behavior has been unsafe or unhealthy, there is a positive impulse behind it. Sometimes it's hard to see the healthy goals hidden within a conflict, but if we can help children express what they really want and need, they are more likely to get to the bottom of the real problem.

★ Focus on children's relationships, rather than any toys or other materials that might be the center of the dispute. Usually, children want to connect with each other but can't figure out how to do it. The toy is often just a symbol of their struggle to balance power and relationship. Is there an activity the children can create together that includes everyone involved in the conflict?

★ Give children the opportunity to propose their own solutions. It's hard for adults to stay out of this, because we have our own ideas about what is fair and what is not. Younger children may need help thinking about and expressing their ideas, but it's important for them to feel as if they participated in coming up with them. And don't forget about the children who weren't involved but were watching—they can contribute valuable ideas, too, if you invite them.

★ Help the group find a solution that everyone can say yes to. Allow them to try out any safe idea they can agree on, even if you don't believe it will work. Sometimes, you will be surprised!

★ Set clear limits on how the problem can be solved. Don't allow children to get their way through insults, threats, exclusion, or violence. Be particularly sensitive to exclusion based on sexism, racism, or other biases. Let children continue to be superhero characters during the discussion, as long as they don't use their roles as an excuse to hurt other people. When someone tries to use inappropriate strategies, point out what they are doing and ask them to try again. "You can't come to my birthday party" is a threat. Don't be afraid to say so.

★ Every single conflict does not require the full conflict resolution process. Sometimes adults can't focus on just a few children. Sometimes children are too tired or hungry to listen effectively. Sometimes they just want to get back to their play, and are fed up with talking. When a lot of children are having conflicts, perhaps it's time to look at your curriculum, your daily routines, and your environment to see if they need to be refreshed. When one child gets into the same kind of fights over and over, perhaps the problem is deeper than her relationship with any one peer, and the answer lies elsewhere.

Teachers can also bring up justice issues by asking appropriate questions when children are playing or creating stories. This can be particularly helpful during superhero play, which often focuses on questions of morality and justice. Is it fair that the monster stole all the money? Is it fair that Catwoman put the bad guy in jail? Is it fair that the Rocketeers are shooting other people with guns? Is it fair that the boys are telling the girls they can't play? Why? The trick is to ask enough questions to stimulate children's thinking without making them feel like you are trying to take over their play or judge it. There is no set rule about this, because some children will welcome your questions and some will be suspicious of them.

Here are some resources that will help you promote peaceful conflict resolution and fairness in your classroom:

Carlsson-Paige, Nancy, and Diane E. Levin. *Before Push Comes to Shove: Building Conflict Resolution Skills with Children.* St. Paul: Redleaf Press, 1998. (This book is out of print, but copies may still be available at www.redleafpress.org, or by searching abebooks.com.)

Evans, Betsy. *You Can't Come to My Birthday: Conflict Resolution with Young Children.* Ypsilanti, MI: High/Scope Press, 2001.

Kreidler, William J., and Sandy Tsubokawa Whittall. *Early Childhood: Adventures in Peacemaking.* 2d ed. Cambridge, MA: Educators for Social Responsibility, 2002.

Pelo, Ann, and Fran Davidson. *That's Not Fair! A Teacher's Guide to Activism with Young Children.* St. Paul: Redleaf Press, 2000.

Slaby, Ron, Wendy C. Roedell, and Diana Arezzo. *Early Violence Prevention: Tools for Teachers of Young Children.* Washington, DC: National Association for the Education of Young Children, 1995.

Smith, Charles A. *The Peaceful Classroom.* Beltsville, MD: Gryphon House, 1993.

Setting Up an Inclusive Classroom

Look around your classroom. Does it reflect the variety of people your children will meet in their lives? Do you actively bring in people who are heroes and heroines that counteract stereotypes and help children feel comfortable with diversity? An inclusive classroom gives an important message to everyone in the classroom community, that fairness is important. When adults exclude or disempower a group of people, either intentionally or unintentionally, they give the message that those people are less than human. When children see those same people being treated unfairly, they will be less able to recognize the problem and less willing to help and be heroic. When children observe that their teachers embrace diversity, they know that everyone will be welcomed and protected.

One of the ways teachers can make sure their classroom is inclusive is to confront stereotypical language they hear in children's superhero play. Teachers have reported young children naming bad guys as Indians, Blacks, Chinamen, Retards, Mexicans, Witches, Homo-fags, and Arabs. Before September 11, 2001, I had never heard anyone called a terrorist in preschool play, but now I have. These labels can be hurtful. Young children rarely understand their meaning, but they know about the fear, anger, and other powerful feelings attached to them.

Many adults look the other way when children use stereotypes because they aren't sure what to say and they don't believe that children mean them, but these words rarely disappear on their own. Teachers should respond quickly to children's stereotypes in their play, and let them know that the words are hurtful and won't be tolerated. Still, it's important to look for the healthy impulse behind even these insulting labels. Children use them for many of the same reasons they get involved in superhero play: to feel powerful, to bond with friends, to explore right and wrong, to have fun, and to express their feelings. Children are more likely to abandon their use of insulting language when adults help them create other words that match their intentions to be powerful, silly, or angry. Here's an example:

> *Teacher, to three children who have been chanting a racist rhyme and giggling: I hear you laughing about those words. They sound funny to you.*
>
> *Abe, age four: Yeah, pee-pee is so funny!*
>
> *Teacher: One of the words I hear is Chinese. Do you know what that means?*
>
> *All: No.*

Eddie, age four: It's a funny word.

Teacher: Actually, it's the name for people from a part of the world called China. I don't think Chinese people like to be talked about that way. I think they would get mad at you.

Nathan, age four: No, we weren't trying to do that.

Teacher: I know, but I won't let you say words that would hurt people's feelings like that. But I can see you're having fun being silly. Can you make up your own silly words?

Eddie: Like shalabalabee?

Teacher: Yes.

Nathan: Like bumble bee bumble bee? (Everyone giggles.)

Eddie: Like poapoapooh? (Everyone laughs.)

Abe: Like finkeefiddle? (Everyone is laughing and falling out of their seats.)

Teacher: Those are great words, and they don't hurt anybody. Do you want me to write them down?

All: Yes!

Several days later, when other children were repeating the rhyme, Eddie told them to say other silly words, because those words would hurt people who were Chinese.

Exclusion based on a person's race, language, ethnicity, or gender is another common tactic children use to feel powerful during superhero play. Gender exclusion, in particular, often goes unchallenged, because it has been accepted for so long. It's true that children often want to play in boy or girl groups as they work out their gender identity, but the view of the opposite sex as aliens or as the enemy only gets worse if adults don't set limits on it. Don't be afraid to name what is happening: "I won't let you hurt people by excluding them just because they are girls. Is there something Ema has to do differently so she can play this game?" Ema's behavior can change; her gender cannot. If Ema hears adults insisting on her right to play, she will feel more comfortable standing up for those rights on her own.

Here are some of the ways teachers can expand children's views about gender and help them resist gender stereotypes:

★ Invite the real world into your classroom. There are any number of healthy ways to be male and female. We tend to reinforce only a narrow range of these options. Expose children to images and examples of men and women who break stereotypes.

★ Look carefully at the books, songs, and stories you are using. Do girls get to be in charge and active? Do boys get to have friendships and help others?

★ Challenge stereotypes by providing new experiences, not through lectures and shaming. Young children's stereotypes are often accurate summaries of their experience. Telling them that they are wrong is an insult to their intelligence. Stick to the facts, and let them come to their own conclusion: "You think only girls can cook, but Aaron's father is a cook. Isn't that interesting!" It can take up to four weeks for a child's opinion to change. Give children time to think, and they will reconsider their beliefs (unless, of course, other people insist that the stereotypes are true).

★ Avoid creating an environment based on gender stereotypes, especially in the dramatic play area. Many schools provide only housekeeping equipment and girl's dress-up clothes. What are some play themes and materials that would attract both genders? Hospital, spaceship, grocery store, bus repair shop, horse stable, and coyote den have been some of my favorites.

★ Are your classroom dolls all babies who spend their time in cribs? Are they all girls, or genderless? Help each doll get a life. Give every one of them a name and gender and family. Treat each one like a member of the class with a full range of interests. Use them to tell stories that break gender lines. I have been successful in getting more boys to play with dolls and more girls to play with large motor equipment this way.

★ Superhero play can reinforce stereotypes, but it can also allow boys and girls to try out behaviors that break those stereotypes. For example, while most children enjoy make-up and fancy clothing, boys over the age of three are often discouraged from wearing anything frilly, silky, flowing, or outrageous. During super-hero play, boys can wear face paint, capes, bracelets, necklaces, and other jewelry without being teased—one teacher made a set of fancy capes from silky and frilly fabrics to see if the boys in her class would wear them, and they loved them.

They can also hug and make body contact with other boys, and admit to being afraid. Likewise, girls can wrestle, develop their large motor skills, and be assertive leaders when they are in a superhero role. Many teachers have told me they have seen more "male" play among girls since the advent of Power Rangers, which had female team members, and Powerpuff Girls. Teachers can encourage these stereotype-breaking activities even when children are not being superheroes, and step in if children are teased.

Insisting that children stop using insulting or exclusionary language does not mean children should not be able to express their curiosity about differences. Preschoolers can make insensitive comments about skin colors, body size, accents, and disabilities. Cutting off their questions because of our own embarrassment gives the impression that the people they are observing are strange or dangerous. Still, children need to learn about social rules. Pointing to a person and saying, "He's so fat!" is rude. I talk to children about the importance of getting people's consent to talk about them: "You're noticing the size of people's bodies. If you want to ask about that person's body, we'll have to get his permission first. Do you want me to help you ask?" I find that children say yes over half the time. I have been surprised at how many people agree to answer children's questions when we ask them for permission—they know that others notice their differences but pretend not to, and they find it refreshing to have someone acknowledge it. Some people say no, and I tell the child that they can't ask any more questions about that person.

Intervening when people are showing bias takes thought and judgment. Most of us never had that modeling when we were young, so we don't trust our own judgments. But if we want children to learn that skill, we have to model it for them. Confronting bias is a heroic act, even for adults!

For more on creating an inclusive community in your classroom, see the following:

Hewitt, Deborah, and Sandra Heidemann. *The Optimistic Classroom: Creative Ways to Give Children Hope.* St. Paul: Redleaf Press, 1998.

Kreidler, William J., and Sandy Tsubokawa Whittall. *Early Childhood: Adventures in Peacemaking.* 2d ed. Cambridge, MA: Educators for Social Responsibility, 2002.

Sapon-Shevin, Mara. *Because We Can Change the World: A Practical Guide to Building Cooperative, Inclusive Classroom Communities.* Upper Saddle River, NJ: Allyn and Bacon, 1998.

Smith, Charles A. *The Peaceful Classroom.* Beltsville, MD: Gryphon House, 1993.

Stone, Jeanette Galambos. *Building Classroom Community: The Early Childhood Teacher's Role.* Washington, DC: National Association for the Education of Young Children, 2002.

York, Stacey. *Big As Life: The Everyday Inclusive Curriculum.* Vol. 1 and 2. St. Paul: Redleaf Press, 1998.

Planning Anti-Bias, Environmental, and Other Community Projects

Classroom routines and activities that reinforce caring and fairness set the stage for heroic deeds in the community—the perfect job for superheroes! Projects that take children out of the classroom broaden their awareness and respect for the lives of others. That awareness allows children to recognize when people need assistance and how to provide it.

Community projects, especially those with an environmental or anti-bias component, help children learn about right and wrong. Superhero play focuses on this same issue, but in the typical superhero story it becomes a physical battle between good and evil. These elements are usually represented by "good guys" and "bad guys," with one side trying to conquer the other using physical prowess, cunning, magic, trickery, and, of course, weapons. We have already seen that these story components symbolize strong emotions that children need to explore. They cannot be banished from children's minds or from their play. But the strategies for "winning" that children learn from these stories are limited, because they tend to focus on destruction of the enemy. With community projects, the focus is on becoming allies, not enemies. Success comes by changing people's minds and fixing the environment so that everyone can feel safe and included.

Teachers don't need to abandon their curriculum plans to create these projects. Sometimes, they just need to take their planning one step further. If a class is studying transportation, the teacher might help the children create a disabled parking place. If the children are pretending to cook, the teacher can plan real cooking projects that reflect the children's home cultures, and end up making simple snacks to give to families when someone is sick. If the class is growing plants, is there a place to scatter native wildflower seeds? Anti-bias and environmental curriculum doesn't require special projects that are separate from the rest of the program. It requires an awareness of opportunities to help others and fight bias, and an eagerness to bring these opportunities into the curriculum on a regular basis. The trick is to find issues and projects that are child-sized, because preschoolers aren't ready to save the whole world—yet.

It's important to plan some community activities that allow children to bond with others. Planting flowers is a good learning project, and can help the community; getting children and their families to plant flowers for someone who would like to grow them but is physically unable connects that learning to real people. Giving children the opportunity to feel strong and useful while creating satisfying relationships at the same time is the most effective way to break the association between power and violence.

Here are some other activities that teachers have used to turn superheroes into real heroes. In your planning, you will have to judge how much your children can do, how many can get involved at one time, and what adult help they will need:

★ Accessibility projects provide many opportunities for children to help others. They are easy for young children to understand and often involve physical activity. If there is someone in your school who uses a wheelchair, walker, cane, or other mobility equipment, ask if he or she will participate in a superhero project. Find a place in your school where the person cannot go because of lack of access. Ask children to plan with the person how to gain access, then let them help change the environment. Look for people in your community who need similar help.

★ Clean up trash around your school, at a local playground, or in a neighbor's yard. Use tongs or rubber gloves. Teach children to sort out the recyclables.

★ Take a group of children to an animal rescue program, and let them help feed and care for the animals.

★ Mark off small observation areas in different environments and visit them regularly. I have used wooden stakes and rope to set aside yard-square areas on a lawn, at the edge of a pond, and in a grove of trees, with signs requesting that the areas not be disturbed. We visited them once a week, took pictures, wrote a journal and brought back plant and seed samples. Butterfly visitors led us into curriculum about protecting habitats and planting flowers for those butterflies.

★ Set up a compost pile and gather lawn clippings and leaves from neighbors, then offer them fresh dirt when it is ready.

★ Offer to help clean someone's sidewalk, steps, or fence. Give everyone a scrub brush. Bring older children into a younger classroom to help wash toys. Combines activism with water play!

Anti-bias, environmental, and community service projects allow young children to get everything they want—power, relationships, and the knowledge that, in their hearts, they are good people. While they may never be powerful enough to conquer all evil, or even all of their fears, they can be valuable, respected members of the community. What more could a superhero want?

For more examples of anti-bias, environmental, and community service curriculum, try these:

Derman-Sparks, Louise, and the ABC Task Force. *Anti-Bias Curriculum: Tools for Empowering Young Children*. Washington, DC: National Association for the Education of Young Children, 1989.

Hall, Nadia Saderman. *Creative Resources for the Anti-Bias Classroom*. Clifton Park, NY: Delmar Learning, 1999.

York, Stacey. *Roots and Wings: Affirming Culture in Early Childhood Programs*. Rev. ed. St. Paul: Redleaf Press, 2003.

Also, on the Internet, take a look at www.rootsforchange.net, the Web site of the Early Childhood Equity Alliance.

STORIES FROM THE CLASSROOM

Bumps

Here's an example of how solving an access problem was incorporated into my classroom's curriculum. It all started with one child's question, "What are these bumpy things?" That led to six weeks of curriculum and a successful community anti-bias project.

The "bumpy things" were the Braille dots attached to the doors all over the college where my center is located. Each afternoon, we took small groups of children on walks. As a child care center on a college campus, we were privileged to have a wide range of interesting experiences available within a safe walking distance. Sometimes these were nature walks to look for tadpoles in a small pond or to collect snips of trees and flowers for art collages. Sometimes we were looking for places that encouraged physical activity, like the running track, soccer fields, or the grassy hill that was perfect for superheroes to roll on. Other times we arranged tours of classrooms and other facilities, such as the photography studio and health clinic.

The bumps that drew the children's attention were on a closet door in a music lab. I thought the children would be fascinated by the electronic equipment, but it didn't hold their attention for long. Our tour guide decided that they could only look and listen, but they weren't allowed to touch anything or make any music. That's a lousy situation for the eager hands of preschoolers! Luckily, young children notice small details that grown-ups take for granted, and the door bumps soon had everyone's interest. On the way back to school, they discovered the bumps on other doors as well.

I asked if anyone knew what they were. No one did. I explained about Braille, but I got blank-faced looks that told me the children were unable to imagine what I was talking about. I decided to pursue the topic.

My staff started planning. I stopped them from jumping directly into the topic of blindness, because I wanted to make sure children understood what sight was before they tried to understand the absence of it. I also wanted to make sure that, if we were going to talk about people, we didn't just focus on their disability.

We brainstormed ways to teach children about vision, and chose a theme we called "How Do People See?" We divided it into three sections:

- How and what do people see?
- What do people use to help themselves see?
- What do people do when they can't see?

We decided to start the first section with a tried-and-true topic — colors. I resisted at first. Lots of teachers do colors curriculum. I do it too, but sometimes I think that its main purpose is to make adults feel like they are teaching something. Most people seem to pick up the names of colors even without the benefit of preschool, so I don't see much reason to spend hours drilling them into children. But in this case, there was already an interest in colors among the children because of the never ending negotiations around Power Rangers colors. Who was blue? Who was pink? Can there be more than one green? Focusing on colors seemed like a good way to bring this discussion into the curriculum and expand it.

When I do talk about colors, I find that children are most interested in the ones with fun names — maroon, lavender, copper, magenta. Some years, I've had emerald and aquamarine Power Rangers. I also like to do treasure hunts for colors inside and out, and get families involved by asking them to bring in items of a particular hue to create color displays. Best of all, colors can lead into other interesting topics, such as skin, hair, and eye colors. With careful planning, color curriculum can end up with five-year-olds looking through magazines to check out the diversity of skin colors included in the pictures.

This time we took the curriculum in a different direction, by exploring the many ways people help themselves see colors. We put magnifying glasses, binoculars, telescopes, and prisms throughout the classroom, along with plastic mirrors, colored filters, and sunglasses. We discussed animals that have "super-vision," like hawks and cats. Some of my superheroes started claiming eagle eyes and X-ray vision.

Then we took a look at eyeglasses. I brought pretend glasses for the doll, Jalen, and told the children a story of how he went to the optometrist and found out he needed glasses to help him see. We gave informal eye tests to all the children, and talked about eye care. I talked about my own experiences with glasses as a young child (my mother was an optometrist, a fact that several children refused to believe), and other adults did too. The one child in the class with glasses didn't say a word for several days, until she carried Jalen to me and said, "I have glasses too!"

These first two sections of the curriculum went on for about three weeks. When we decided that the children had a good idea about how they used their eyes, I asked children the question, "Can you think of a time when you can't use your eyes to see?" The first response, "At night," was first greeted with enthusiasm by most of them, but others questioned it.

"You can still see the moon," someone said.

"Not if you're asleep," another child said.

"But then you can see your dreams."

"But that's in your head."

"What if you were in a dark, dark room with no light anywhere?"

"You could use a flashlight."

After circle, we got out flashlights and set up a cardboard box with a blanket over it to keep out the light. Some children enjoyed getting in with no flashlight; others refused to get in the box, even with a light.

"You don't have to get in the box to see darkness," one child said. "Just close your eyes."

Some children tried it, but a few said they could still see light, even with their eyes closed.

"We could wear a blindfold!" a child shouted. Not everyone knew what that was, so she explained. Some children were willing to try it, and some were not.

"That's an interesting word," I said. "It has the word *blind* in it. Does anyone know what that means?"

A few children did. "You can't see!" they said.

"Not even with glasses or a flashlight?" someone asked.

"No, because your eyes don't work," a four-year-old said.

"Has anyone ever met a person who is blind?" I asked. No one had. I let them know that I had invited a new person, Annie, to visit the school, and that she liked music, reading, and running, and that she was blind.

When I ask someone to be an "example" for my curriculum, I don't want the children to think of that person in only one way—as blind, or as a carpenter, or as a senior citizen. I ask the person beforehand for three things he or she would like the children to know about them and focus on those.

"But how will she get here?" a child asked.

"She has a helper named Merlin. Merlin is a dog who knows how to help Annie get around. He's called a *service dog.* "

"Can he talk?" someone said.

"I don't think so. I've never met a talking dog," I said.

That week, we put out books that included service dogs and people who were blind. I talked a lot about how Annie would come to play her guitar, that she would bring a book to read, and that she would show us how she runs. I also brought a new kind of book that I had borrowed, a book in Braille. A few children remembered the bumps they had found on the door.

When Annie came, the children fell in love with Merlin, even a few who had been afraid of dogs in the past. One wanted Merlin to wear his superhero cape, but Annie said no. They were fascinated with the harness Annie held while they walked together, and Annie let two children at a time take short turns walking with her and Merlin. She played several songs on her guitar, showed us how Merlin helped her run, and read from the Braille book, a book about dogs.

Annie brought two other items, a fold-up cane and a Braille typewriter. The children set up several block barriers, and Annie showed how she used the cane to navigate past them. Then she sat at the typewriter and typed out the alphabet. She had already typed out the names of all the children, and she handed them out before she and Merlin said good-bye.

For the next few days, the children used wooden dowels to help themselves find their way through obstacle courses. We made harnesses, and children pretended to be service dogs, leading other children around the play-ground. After they got used to the canes and harnesses, several of the oldest children tried moving with their eyes closed. A couple were willing to put on blindfolds.

On our next walk, the children looked for Braille on every door. I asked if they knew what the dots said. One child figured it out—the dots gave the number of the room. The children noticed Braille on several signs as well.

Then we came to a door with no Braille. The children looked at me, puzzled. "Hey," one of them said, "that's not fair."

"It's not fair!" the others said.

When I'm doing anti-bias-related curriculum, that's the response that tells me I'm on the right track. "Why is that?" I said.

"If a blind person came here, she wouldn't know what room this is," a child said, and everyone agreed.

"What should we do?" I asked.

"We have to get new numbers!" they shouted, and they wanted to do it right away.

I had to do some research. The door numbers were made out of brass, and would take months to order. We had found several other doors without numbers, and the children were impatient. Young children can't wait that long for action. I asked Annie to come back with her Braille typewriter.

We made a list of the missing room numbers, and Annie typed them up. The children helped cut them out, and we taped them to the doors.

"Hooray, we did it!" they shouted.

"You really are heroes and heroines," I said.

When we got back to the classroom, I gave everyone medals. We made two more special medals and presented them to Annie and Merlin.

What impressed me about the children who participated in this project was that they quickly learned to view Annie as a normal human being, rather than an oddity, yet they maintained their awareness of her differences and recognized she needed special accommodations that they themselves didn't require. They were able to translate that awareness into a concern for people they had never even met—other blind people who might need to know the room numbers on campus. They were able to figure out what they could do to help, even though no one demanded they do it. That's true heroism to me.

CHAPTER 7

Working with Families and Staff

"I'm afraid to talk to parents about superhero play. I know I'll get a million opinions, and nobody will agree. Even my staff can't agree. I'm the head teacher. Can't I just decide what the rules are?"

—Rosa, teacher in a four- and five-year-old classroom

WHEN TEACHERS ARE supporting children's ideas about superhero play, they also have to pay attention to the needs and beliefs of families and other staff. Teachers like Rosa can't satisfy everyone when they set up their policies, because parents and staff often have many different opinions about the play. They can, however, listen to parents and let them share their experiences and values, and work with staff to create a consistent approach to the play. When everyone is in basic agreement about the program's goals and rules, teachers are more likely to succeed at transforming superhero play.

Teachers can work with their families and staff in these ways:
- ★ Listening to families
- ★ Sharing information with families about the media
- ★ Negotiating and planning with staff
- ★ Clarifying how your staff approaches gender issues

Listening to Families

It's easy to overlook parents' ideas about superheroes. Many teachers are so eager to share their expertise with families that they forget to listen. That can give the impression that teachers think they know more about the children than their families do. While teachers usually understand more about child development, parents know more about their own children, their history, and their culture. As professionals, we should take the lead in listening to parents, rather than expecting them to always listen to us first. You will have a better chance of gaining parent support for your superhero policies if you show that their opinions and experiences are taken into account.

Many parents have strong feelings about guns, war, television, and superhero games, and how they should be handled in the classroom. Some are opposed to the play, and some in favor. Many are ambivalent, and want your guidance. Others haven't thought about the topic much, or don't consider it a problem.

When I hear a lot of disagreement among parents about superhero play, I go back to a goal everyone can support: no one wants their child to grow up violent. Of course, parents don't always have the same idea of what that means. For one family, being violent includes being a soldier or using a gun for hunting. For others, being a soldier is an honor, hunting is a wholesome sport, and violence is an important option to have when you are attacked. However, I have always gotten everyone to agree that, within the walls of my classroom, violence is not an option that will be tolerated. Sometimes that agreement is limited, as it was with Gary, the parent of a three-year-old:

Gary: I don't want you teaching my son not to fight back. I don't want other kids pushing him around. I want him to fight back.

Teacher: I don't want kids pushing him around either. Have you seen teachers let that happen?

Gary: He says Cal hit him, and he hit back, and you stopped him.

Teacher: Yes, I did.

Gary: So how is he supposed to defend himself?

Teacher: I helped him say very clearly that Cal had to stop. I could tell he was pretty angry, so I let him scream it as loud as he could. I helped Cal back off, then I helped them solve the problem. They both wanted the same cape. They figured out how to get another one, and they went off and played together. They're friends. I don't see any reason to let a fistfight continue when kids can solve problems with words.

Gary: Words are fine, but he's not going to always have you around to help.

Teacher: True. I can't say he's never going to need to fight, but do you really want him to think he can punch people in a classroom?

Gary: No, not really. He'll just get in trouble.

Teacher: I know there are places in the world where he might have to fight, but not at school. I don't let anybody do that here, but I always help kids stand up for themselves.

Gary: Okay, I don't mind telling him not to fight at school, but I don't want you telling him he should never fight.

Teacher: I don't like encouraging kids to fight anywhere, but I'm only in charge here in my classroom. I'm willing to say he has to use words at school. If you

(continued on page 174)

Parents can have a wide range of opinions on superhero play. Here are some samples from workshops and meetings I have led on the subject:

"I don't have a problem with superhero play. I did it when I was a kid, and I'm a pacifist now." —*father of a four-year-old*

"It's just what boys do. They like that superhero stuff, especially the shooting. I don't like it, but you can't stop it." —*mother of a three-year-old*

"GI Joe scares me. They're trying to teach my baby to march off to war." —*mother of a three-year-old*

"Everybody wants to get rid of guns, even toy guns. I grew up hunting, and I'm going to teach my kids how to hunt as soon as they're old enough to understand how to handle a gun safely. If I had my way, I'd give every kid a toy gun and teach them how to respect it." —*father of a two-year-old*

"I grew up hunting too. I'm a vet. I have guns. But some of this superhero stuff is too much. I don't want my boy thinking he can walk around spraying bullets at anybody he thinks is the enemy. When he gets mad at me, he starts shooting me with his finger, and I make him stop. Nobody points a gun at me, not even a pretend one. I know what they can do. It's not a joke, and it's not a game." —*father of a four-year-old*

"Just let it go. They'll use up a lot of energy and they won't hurt anybody. Why get all bent out of shape about it. It's pretend, for God's sake." —*mother of a five-year-old*

"My cousin was murdered by some jerk who thought killing made him a man. My son didn't see that, thank God, but he's heard all about it. Don't tell me I should let him play that out." —*father of a four-year-old*

"Gun play breeds killers." —*mother of a four-year-old*

"Looks like fun to me." —*mother of a three-year-old*

> *tell him the same thing, I think the rules will be clearer for him.*
>
> *Gary: I can do that. But I will teach him how to fight when teachers aren't around.*

Making sure everyone understands your basic stance on violence in the classroom provides an important safety net when discussions get heated and adults start attacking each other's integrity. I have had one mother accuse another of promoting violence by supporting superhero play. That parent responded by calling the first a "pacifist wimp" who was destroying our country's willingness to fight for itself. Another time, a father said that people who won't let boys play with guns want them to be like girls. I could almost see the steam coming out of the ears of several people in the audience. Those are the times when it's valuable to step back and help everyone remember that we're all aiming for the same thing, even if we can't agree on how to get there.

Don't expect to get everyone to agree with every one of your policies. The goal is to keep a dialogue going that will help the parents and teachers learn more about each other's ideas and help the child understand that rules at home might be different from rules at school. Some parents won't be pleased with your choices, and you will have to decide how much you are willing to change your program to satisfy them. Occasionally, you may have to work with a family to find another program that is a better match for their values.

Here is a conversation I recorded with Adella, mother of four-year-old Bradley, about his superhero play. It was one of a series of dialogues we had that resulted in new ideas for activities at school and a willingness on her part to let her son participate in superhero play:

> *Adella: You said at the parent meeting that you wanted to know how parents feel about gun play at school. Well, I don't let Bradley play with guns, and I don't like the X-Men game he's playing. I don't want him to think violence is okay, whether it's pretend or not. I've noticed you let them play with guns here, and I wish you wouldn't.*
>
> *Teacher: You're right, I do let them do play superheroes here, and I let them pretend to use weapons. We don't let children bring toys from home, including weapons.*
>
> *Adella: I don't mind the superhero stuff, but they all*

have guns and all sorts of weapons these days. I don't let him watch those shows anymore, but he gets to watch at his dad's. His dad just doesn't care. He buys him toys that look real, like real guns. I won't let him bring them into my house. I don't mind swords so much, but guns give me the creeps. I don't even let him watch the news.

Teacher: So you don't really want him to pretend to play with guns, but other weapons are okay?

Adella: Well, I don't really want him to do any of it, but I think if you take it all away, they'll just want it more.

Teacher: That's been my experience too.

Adella: I wish it would just go away.

Teacher: What do you think Bradley gets out of playing with guns?

Adella: It makes him feel grown-up. Like that's the way a man's supposed to be. That's scary. He saw his dad hit me. I don't want him to grow up that way.

Teacher: You want him to be respectful.

Adella: I don't want him to think that's how you treat people, that you can just hurt them.

Teacher: Do you think that's what he's learning by playing with weapons?

Adella: I think that's what the TV shows are teaching him. What do you think?

Teacher: I see him playing pretty carefully, pretty safely. Bradley is trying to be a leader of the older boys group, and that's a game where he feels he can take charge.

Adella: He's always talking about those kids. And he shows me some of his kicks and things. It's a little scary, but he seems to be able to do it safely. Does he hurt people?

Teacher: No, that group is pretty safe. Bradley has a

good idea of his physical limits, much more than last year. He's very coordinated, and they do lots of gymnastics when they are playing. That lets him be a leader. I think he's learned to be safe, partly from his play.

Adella: He's always been much more coordinated than his brother Erin was at the same age. It's funny, I wasn't as worried about Erin because he wasn't into the TV so much.

Teacher: I also think those kids feel much more powerful when they carry play weapons.

Adella: I want him to feel powerful, but couldn't they use something else? Like magic wands?

Teacher: That's a good idea. My goal is always to help them find other ways to be powerful. I find that if we just take the guns away, from our point of view we're teaching them to be safe, but from their point of view, we're telling them they can't feel powerful.

Adella: Yeah, I can see that. Then he would want it even more, like you said at the meeting.

Teacher: What do you think would work for Bradley? Do you think magic wands would appeal to him?

Adella: It's not a gun. Probably not. I don't want him to feel like he can't be with his friends. Can you get them to shoot magic spells instead of bullets, or something like that?

Teacher: We could try that. We could try to add some other magic components to the play. Maybe some magic spells, or some magic tricks with his body. He loves to throw his body all around. . . .

Adella: Oh, Lord, he does that everywhere.

Teacher: We could make some of that into magic motions. Something magic could happen when he does a gymnastics trick. Something a little different from the X-Men stories. I really think he's ready to expand those stories, to help make up his own.

*Adella: We could do it at home too. I avoid talking
about the X-Men because I hate them. And because he
does it at his dad's, and that makes me furious. That's
not Bradley's problem.*

*Teacher: If you write down an X-Men story of his and
bring it to school, I can read it to the class if he wants.
It might start a whole new story going.*

*Adella: That would be great. Can I tell him he has to
write a story with no guns in it?*

*Teacher: You have to decide. I would be very careful.
You could tell him why you don't like guns, but I think
in the long run, he has to decide.*

Adella: I could tell him only pretend guns are okay.

*Teacher: Let me know how it goes. And let me know if
you have any other ideas about how I can help
Bradley.*

Adella: Thanks.

There may be times when you decide to restrict superhero play based on what you
hear from parents. Some of the stories you hear will be painful. There are families that
have had direct and horrific experiences with weapons and who have lost relatives and
friends to violence. There are schools that have large war refugee populations, or are in
neighborhoods where guns are used to kill people regularly. Some children have witnessed these events. Superhero and weapons play has a very different meaning for
these families. They don't view gun play as the children's attempt to symbolize and
work out feelings. They see their children imitating adult behavior, and it scares them.
These family members can feel traumatized by the play and want it stopped.

My experiences with parents have helped me realize that there is not one correct way
to react to superhero play. Its meaning can't be taken out of its cultural context. The
way we respond has to take those circumstances into account. And while I firmly believe
that all children can use guided superhero play to successfully explore their needs and
feelings, I also know that teachers should not try to be therapists. There are children and
adults who are emotionally at risk from superhero play, particularly play that involves
weapons. In those situations, classroom policies may have to be more restrictive. Even if

I don't ban superhero play, I have to provide very firm limits and a clear explanation to the families of how I ensure that real violence will not be tolerated.

Sharing Information with Families about the Media

Many teachers are concerned about the influence of TV, movies, and advertising on children's play. They worry that the violence, stereotyping, competition, and emphasis on commercial toys distort children's social relationships in the classroom. I have heard over and over, "I wish kids wouldn't watch that stuff at home." But most of children's media exposure isn't under teacher control. Parents are the ones who decide. If teachers want children to become thoughtful users of the media, they have to work with families.

Sometimes, though, in our rush to advocate for what we believe is best, we end up trying to tell parents what to do and shame them into action. It rarely works. Family members can end up resenting a teacher's intrusion if there is no sense of partnership based on mutual trust.

When it comes to media use, there can be a wide range of practices among the families in a classroom. One family may think nothing of taking their preschooler on family outings to the latest gory horror film, leaving the TV on at all times, or filling up their child's closet with toy guns and bombs. Another may provide a limited selection of videos their children can watch, and allow Grandma to buy a plastic weapon or two. Another may refuse to allow children to watch any TV or movies at all, and won't allow any war toys in the house. One family may use the TV as an occasional reward for good behavior, and another may rely on it as a daily babysitter. In many families, it's adults who like having the TV turned on for hours at a time. Each family has its own set of beliefs, needs, and routines. The way a family uses the media can't be separated easily from the way they have structured their lives. Suggestions about how to use TV aren't helpful when they don't take the whole family situation into account.

A typical approach is to tell families they should watch less TV. It's an excellent idea. The American Academy of Pediatrics, along with numerous other organizations, condemns media violence and recommends keeping children under age two away from TV altogether. But what is best for young children may not be what works in a family that has other needs to balance, particularly if there are older children in the home. People have so many time pressures and so many authorities telling them how to be better parents that they often protect themselves by shutting out the information. Just telling families to stop what they are doing is like telling children "no"—they are not likely to succeed unless they have realistic alternatives that meet their needs. Parents who set their children in front of the TV so they can get dinner on the table or take a moment to recover from work won't pay any attention to advice that threatens to disrupt their entire evening routine. They will only feel disrespected by those giving the advice.

Teachers should gather as much information as they can about the effects of the media on children. There are numerous reasons children should be spending less time sitting passively and staring at a screen, and there are alternatives that will actively help children develop physically, mentally, and socially. But before you start preaching to parents, you should set aside all your knowledge and listen. What are the issues and concerns parents have about the media and superhero play? How do families use the TV? How do the adults use it in their own lives? What do they like about TV, and what would they change? Have they tried to modify their family routines? What has worked for them, and what has not? Instead of a lecture at a parent meeting, have a conversation, with parents doing most of the talking. Let them describe their own perspective, but help them avoid telling others what to do.

One of the biggest surprises I've had in talking to parents about the media came when Aretha, a single mother of three children, described what had worked for her family. She said that her problems decreased when her children increased their TV watching! What changed was how they watched it. Before, she would turn on the TV whenever she needed to get housework done, or when she was tired or angry. It didn't matter what shows were on—cartoons, game shows, soap operas, sitcoms. Jenna, age two and a half, didn't understand much of what she was seeing and just wanted to be with her mother. Chas, age ten, was bored and had other shows he wanted to watch, but they were on at times when the TV was turned off. Howard, age six, wanted everyone else to stay quiet so he could watch whatever was on.

"It wasn't working," Aretha said. "The baby kept interrupting me, the oldest kept complaining and teasing the middle one, who would whine. They were driving me nuts. I probably wouldn't have changed anything if my kids were the passive types, but they're not."

She decided to let the older children have more control of the situation. She started by talking to the ten-year-old. He felt he was too old for some of the "baby cartoons." He wanted to watch more mature programs, but he didn't like the soaps or comedies that relied on sex talk. He wanted adult action shows, like *Star Trek*. They picked out a few shows that were on his list that would also work for his younger brother. Only one was during the time Aretha normally turned on the TV.

"At first I resisted, but then I decided to see if I could change my schedule to match theirs. I started doing more of my housework during the show times they wanted. That would have been fine, except for Jenna. She still wanted to be with me."

Aretha made a deal with her other two children. They could add on another show to watch as long as they got their homework done. In exchange, they would stay with the two-year-old for up to an hour while she made dinner. They agreed, reluctantly. But after a few days, they were enjoying the time. They got very involved in playing. "They got to be little kids again, building with blocks, drawing, playing with cars. It was like they had forgotten how to play. The TV was off. And Jenna loved the attention." They would still get into fights, but less than before.

The last part of the routine that changed turned out to be the most important to Aretha. "I like *Star Trek,* so I would do things like fold laundry, and the kids would

help. Watching the shows together was the best thing I ever did. We would complain about how tacky some of the costumes were, or how they used special effects to shoot a scene. I remember you said something about helping children understand what they were watching, how important that was. I would ask if they knew how they filmed some of the space shots. Chas knew a lot about it, but I was surprised at how little Howard understood. Jenna started asking lots of questions. Sometimes Chas would get mad, because she wouldn't stop, so we made a rule about only asking questions during commercials."

The two oldest started noticing how animation and other film techniques were used in toy commercials. "They would sit and analyze what was real and what wasn't in the ads. It became an intellectual challenge for them. They got quite skeptical about the ads, which was fine with me."

Aretha wasn't sure what the youngest was getting out of it. "I'm sure she is picking up some of it, but the important thing is that it's a family activity. Jenna doesn't whine so much, she does more listening and watching. She likes being around everybody. She always has, I just forgot about it."

Aretha started watching other shows with the children as well. "I was kind of appalled. Some of the cartoons were so violent. I didn't really want Jenna watching it, so I decided to be just with her outside during that time. I had to think about what I could cook on those days that I could just pop in the oven and leave."

Aretha was proud of the changes she instituted. The children still have fights over what to watch, she still gets frazzled, and the toddler still wants to grab her leg sometimes when she is on the phone or cooking, but overall, the family routines had become much less stressful.

"I feel like the TV went from being a bad babysitter to being a good educational experience, even when the shows weren't very good. And I know my children feel better about the whole thing."

Aretha's story helped me realize that each family has to handle TV and other media in their own way. We can be advocates for children and a resource for parents, but we can't tell them what to do. Here is some of the information that, in my experience, parents have found useful:

- ★ The most valuable thing you can do to help children understand the media is to help them slow down and think about what they have experienced and what they are feeling. TV show producers don't like that—children might stop watching! If your child doesn't want to stop the show, skip the commercials. Establish a routine of muting commercials and asking questions about what happened during the show segment. "That looked scary to me. Was it scary for you?" "I didn't understand that part. What was happening?"

- ★ Let children control the Off button. Most children don't realize they can turn away from scenes that scare them. Give them permission to walk out of a movie or turn off the set if it is too scary. If others are watching and the child can't turn off the TV, let them know that you will help them move away and you will stay with them. Sometimes, we get so caught up in the plot ourselves that we don't want to leave! Make yourself do it for your child.

- ★ You get to set the rules about TV use in your home, but your children may have strong feelings about the rules you set. Don't ignore those feelings; listen to them. Children may have other ideas for how to meet your concerns while getting what they want. Learning to compromise and take other people's views into account are important lessons for children.

- ★ Videos are a useful alternative to TV for many families. You can prescreen them and they aren't interrupted by commercials. Children like to watch the same video over and over so they can take the time to understand what they are seeing and feeling. They like to be able to predict what will happen next. That can drive adults crazy, but it's better for children. Other parents can probably recommend videos that will work for your family.

- ★ Some children laugh when they are very scared. Others get very still. Don't assume that your child is understanding or enjoying a scary scene—ask them.

- ★ Model taking deep breaths, moving around, and stretching to relax during high-action shows.

★ Some children are more sensitive to sensory stimulation than others. Even if one of your children enjoys a particular show, another one (even one who is older) might be frightened by it.

★ Don't allow older children to tease someone who is afraid of a TV show or movie. Support each child's ability to be aware of his own feelings and keep himself safe.

★ When we stop children from talking during a movie or show, the message we are giving is that the show is more important than the child's feelings and questions. If your child is too disruptive to be in a movie theater, it's probably better to wait until he or she is older.

★ When characters solve a problem using violence, help children think about other ways the problem can be solved. If your child is too young to imagine alternatives, they are probably too young to watch the show, even if your child begs you to see it again.

★ If you let your children watch a scary show, expect them to incorporate what they are seeing into their play. If you don't like their play, it's better to stop watching the show than to stop the play.

★ Children pay attention to whatever is on the TV. They may not act like they are listening when the news is on, but they are. Many news shows give an inaccurate picture of the world by focusing on violence, crime, and celebrity activities. Is that the image of humanity you want your child to internalize?

★ Sometimes, children love to do something other than watch TV. They just don't know how to ask. Crayons and paper, blocks, climbing a tree, helping clean the floor—you would be surprised how much happier children can be when they don't have to sit still.

★ If your child gets a toy that doesn't work as expected, talk about how frustrating it is to see a toy in an ad or on a package that can't be used as advertised. Help the child take the toy back and complain. You will be modeling how to take action against injustice.

★ If you don't want friends and relatives buying certain kinds of toys for your children, let them know before the holiday or the birthday comes around. That may start an argument, but it's easier to resolve the conflict before the child has the toy in hand. Then it becomes an argument between you and your child.

★ It's okay for children to be bored sometimes. You don't have to solve the problem by turning on the TV. Give them some open-ended play materials like art supplies, boxes, plastic containers, and yarn, and let them create their own excitement.

★ If you're not sure what to do, talk to other parents. They have probably had the same problem, or know someone else who has. Help set up a bulletin board where parents can share media information and experiences—what has worked for them and what has not.

Here are some resources on media awareness and alternatives to TV:

Cantor, Joanne. *"Mommy, I'm Scared": How TV and Movies Frighten Children and What We Can Do to Protect Them.* San Diego: Harcourt, 1998.

Hoffman, Eric. *Changing Channels: Activities Promoting Media Smarts and Creative Problem Solving for Kids.* St. Paul: Redleaf Press, 2002.

Levin, Diane E. *Remote Control Childhood? Combating the Hazards of Media Culture.* Washington, DC: National Association for the Education of Young Children, 1998.

Steyer, James. *The Other Parent: The Inside Story of the Media's Effect on Our Children.* New York: Atria Books, 2002.

Walsh, David Allen. *Dr. Dave's Cyberhood.* New York: Simon and Schuster, 2001.

---

www.aap.org/advocacy/mmcamp.htm—"Media Matters: A National Media Education Campaign" from the American Academy of Pediatrics

www.medialit.org—Center for Media Literacy

www.kidsfirst.org—Kids First!

www.limitv.org—LimiTV, Inc.

www.lionlamb.org—The Lion and Lamb Project

www.media-awareness.ca—Media Awareness Network

Negotiating and Planning with Staff

Teachers have the same range of opinions on superhero play as parents. When staff get together to decide their superhero play policies, they tend to skip discussing these differences to get to the rule-making stage. But listening to each other first is important. How does each staff member feel about superhero play? What experiences have led them to those beliefs? As in conflict resolution for children, adults should listen to each other's points of view and acknowledge their differences before trying to solve the problem.

When I did a staff training at one school where the staff had asked for help setting up superhero play rules, the teachers were surprised when they talked to each other—some teachers wanted to have a total ban on superhero play, some wanted to let children play the game but not with any weapons. Some only objected to toy guns. Others saw no reason to ban play that was clearly fun for the children. Here are some of their comments:

> *"I get very sad when I see children shooting each other with guns, and I get scared thinking about what would happen if they were using real guns."*

> *"These children are innocent, and they don't know what they're imitating when they pick up a toy gun. It's just another way our society makes boys part of the war machine."*

> *"There's nothing wrong with being a soldier. My son played with guns, and my husband was a soldier, and they are both very respectful people."*

> *"I don't care if kids do this at home. When they're in a big group at school, the play gets too dangerous."*

> *"I would rather tell kids they can't use guns, only magic wands."*

> *"No, they'll just use the magic wands to shoot each other when you're not looking."*

> *"I don't like the play, but I don't think we should make rules just based on our own feelings. The children really like it, and I don't see them hurting each other any more than they do in their other play."*

After making a list of possible policies, the staff I was working with came up with these guidelines in their second meeting:

★ Each classroom staff will choose an inside area for dramatic play (not every classroom had one) and set up themes that reflect the interests of the children in the class. They will make sure parents know about these themes and make an effort to include parents in any curriculum that supports the theme. When staff members see children interested in superhero play, they will work together to set up a theme that everyone can support.

★ Superhero and weapon play will be allowed on the preschool playground (a space shared by four classrooms) around the climbing structure and on the deck nearby. Quieter superhero play can take place in the playhouse and sandbox. However, no superhero play will be allowed when the two-year-olds are on the playground.

★ Children can pretend they are commercial characters, but staff will not set up curriculum that uses commercial characters. Children can wear clothing with commercial images, but no toy weapons or superhero props from home will be allowed. The director will put out a newsletter explaining why these items have caused problems in the past and asking for parents help in keeping them at home.

★ No weapon play will be allowed indoors, and no inside toys will be allowed outdoors for use as weapons. Children can make weapons using art materials outdoors. Staff from all classrooms will cooperate to create a quiet area on the outside patio that will work for art projects. Teachers will let each other know what kinds of projects they are planning, so the other classrooms can decide if they want to participate.

They also discussed what the teachers could say to introduce the new policies and bring up their concerns about superhero play with the children. I cautioned the staff on making changes too quickly, and had them set priorities. I have found that it's better to start with small modifications that can be successful and that the children can understand. Too much change all at once can cause tremendous anxiety for some children, and can result in a lot of rule testing and regression. The consequences of new policies can't always be predicted, and it's easier to correct your course when the changes have been small scale. Building on successes while recognizing the value of making small mistakes allows everyone to grow together.

When I checked back with the director six months later, she said that most of the policies had been implemented. Families were supportive, and most of the children had accepted the changes. There was a lot of superhero play going on among the oldest children but they were doing it safely, and some of the teachers were picking up the idea of supporting the play with other curriculum. The idea the staff had come up with about outdoor art projects had not worked well, because the school's intricate schedule for sharing the playground made it hard to set them up. Some of the teachers had started allowing children to build paper weapons inside, but only allowing them to be used outside.

As with parents, it's important to remember that your superhero policies won't please every staff member, but they should be guidelines that everyone is willing to follow. Otherwise, the rules will gradually be undermined, and children will need to test everyone to figure out who is really in charge. When teachers have shared how they feel about superhero play with each other, are willing to respect their differences, and forge a compromise solution that they can enforce consistently, everyone ends up more satisfied.

Clarifying How Your Staff Approaches Gender Issues

Parents and teachers bring up the differences between boys and girls in every class and workshop I do on superhero play. Preschoolers want to know more about gender roles, and superhero play is one of the activities children use to play out and often exaggerate what they have learned. Some people believe the differences are learned through a huge number of hidden cultural messages, and want to know how to lessen this gap:

> *What can I do to get my daughter to show more interest in running around and climbing and less interest in clothes? I know it's not just because she's a girl. I'm a girl, and I'm a carpenter. I don't go around in frilly overalls. I can't believe how society controls them so early.* —Cassandra, mother of four-year-old Alice

Others believe the differences are genetic and reflect our evolutionary past. They talk about the futility of efforts to change the stereotypes:

> *I don't know where he learned that [shooting at his friends with his finger]. We don't watch TV. We raised him just like his sister, and she never did that. It must really be genetic.* —Samantha, mother of two-year-old Joshua

Before teachers can help families and children think through their ideas on masculinity and femininity, they have to be aware of their own attitudes and experiences. What do you believe about gender differences? What experiences have shaped your views? How do you react to children who are playing out gender stereotypes? How do you feel about play that excludes by gender?

These questions reflect a debate about men and women that has been going on in the United States for a long time. When I started working with young children in the early seventies, the popular belief (or, perhaps, the hope) was that boys and girls were basically the same, and that the ways we respond to children determine the differences we see in their behavior. If we would just treat everyone the same, gender distinctions would disappear. In the last thirty years, many of the differences in gender roles have faded, and it has become clear that, given the chance, women are quite capable of many tasks traditionally assigned to men, from changing lightbulbs to playing basketball to running a country. And men are able to change diapers, do laundry, and talk about feelings when they stop avoiding it.

However, researchers have also completed a long list of studies documenting differences in behavior, brain structure, and body chemistry between males and females. These studies, along with the frustration of parents and teachers who found gender differences far more difficult to erase than they expected, have pushed the pendulum sharply to the opposite view, that evolution and genetics can explain practically every difference we see. I believe people on both sides of this controversy have allowed politics to get far in front of the scientific evidence; we are just beginning to understand how biology and experience combine to create what we think of as male and female behavior.

So when Samantha labels her son Joshua's gun play as genetic, what does she mean? For many people, saying that a behavior is genetic means, "There's nothing we can do to change it." But is the act of shooting really hardwired into Joshua's male body? Handguns were invented in the fifteenth century; no prehistoric toddlers ever ran around shooting out of their fingertips. So even if his mother isn't aware of it, Joshua must have learned those motions and heard those bang-bang sounds somewhere.

Still, Joshua was more likely than his sister to pay attention and learn those motions and sounds. Before guns, children threw rocks and sticks, shot pretend arrows, and swung pretend swords, and boys undoubtedly did it more than girls. There may very well be genetic reasons why boys are attracted to weaponry and fighting more than girls. If the theorists are to be believed, boys have a greater need for status and physical dominance, while girls focus more on empathy and friendships—the two sides of the struggle to balance power and relationship. We can't ignore these drives, but that doesn't mean we have to buy into the images of boys as violent "alpha males" and girls as passive victims that so many cultures and so many superhero shows and toys promote. The actual behaviors we see are most certainly learned, and every culture has different visions of how boys and girls are expected to act. If we model respectful ways to gain status and maintain relationships, then that's what both boys and girls will imitate. Will that completely eliminate violence, particularly male violence? Of course not. But I believe that both males and females can learn to meet their needs in ways that are assertive yet nonviolent, even if their needs are different.

What motivates boys to shoot finger bullets and wear Superman underwear? What attracts girls to wicked witches and poison soups? I asked students in one of the adult classes I teach to help me make a list of possibilities. Here's what they came up with for young boys:

- ★ Power
- ★ Independence
- ★ Control and dominance
- ★ Overcoming fear and other emotions without having to express them directly
- ★ Status
- ★ Bravery
- ★ Danger
- ★ Violence
- ★ Competition
- ★ Anything that involves a lot of physical action and strength
- ★ Whatever they see other males doing

And for young girls:

- ★ Relationships
- ★ Interdependence
- ★ Whatever helps them express fear and other emotions
- ★ Safety
- ★ Attractiveness
- ★ Feeling useful
- ★ Whatever they see other females doing

When I asked them to vote, most chose either violence or status as the likely impetus for boys, but for girls, they chose "whatever they see other females doing." One of them summed it up this way: "Men make things happen and mess things up so they can end up on top; women stay in the background and pick up the pieces." Note that all the students in the class were women. I found it fascinating that they viewed men's motivation as genetic and beyond control, while they saw their own behavior as learned.

The research that will give us definite answers about what is and is not genetic in males and females hasn't been done, but enough data has already been collected to give teachers some guidance in the classroom. Studies show clearly that, regardless of any differences between the average male and female, there is a huge overlap between the genders on all measures of personality and behavior, especially in young children. Focusing on gender differences might make sense when comparing large groups, but in the early childhood classroom, teachers should be committed to promoting each child's development as an individual and as a member of the classroom community. Knowing children's genders will affect teachers' decisions, but not nearly as much as their knowledge of each child's personality, family, and culture.

Here are some of the lessons I have learned about gender from watching children in American preschools for the past thirty years:

★ Children want to know whether they are a boy or a girl.

★ After age two and a half, they tend to model their behavior on people of their own gender.

★ If they see an activity done only by people of the opposite sex, some conclude they shouldn't do it.

★ If teachers expose children to people who contradict their stereotypes, children will gradually change their beliefs and behavior.

★ Both boys and girls are interested in balancing autonomy and relationship; more boys are attracted to strategies that gain them power and dominance, while more girls like strategies that lead to interdependence and preserve relationships, but there are so many exceptions to this rule that it is almost useless as a guide to individual children.

★ Many children do not fit the prevailing gender stereotypes, and they often feel bad about themselves for being different by the time they enter elementary school.

★ If violence is common in the environment, boys are more likely to learn to use it than girls.

★ While boys are more likely to imitate violence, it is not inborn, either in boys or in girls, but a widely used strategy for gaining power that can be unlearned when better methods are made available.

★ Viewing boys and girls as opposites can blind us to the many similarities between boys and girls, and to the wide variation in personalities, interests, and commu-nication styles within each gender. I prefer to see the genders as two different versions of the same image, like the overlapping parts of a stereoscopic picture, the kind that appears three-dimensional. If the two are made identical, if one overpowers the other, or if they are pulled too far apart, the picture loses its depth and beauty.

Sadly, many boys see the men in their lives and in the media expressing their manliness through violence. That's an easy answer to the question of how to be a man—it looks powerful and brave, it's very physical, and it forces people to do what you want. Likewise, many girls see women who are dependent, abused, or appreciated only for their sexuality. That's what children imitate when they create their superhero stories. If we believe that being male means being violent and that being female means being helpless, we will reinforce those beliefs in the classroom. If we view those actions as strategies that children have learned to express their underlying needs for power and relationships, then we can challenge and change the behaviors, as long as we don't ignore what they need.

One of the reasons I have focused on superhero play in my teaching is that, even though it often starts from a place that exaggerates violence and gender stereotypes, it gives me the chance to guide children toward a more hopeful, nonviolent path. That isn't easy when the rest of the culture celebrates using violence as a tool for power, especially for boys, but it makes my job worthwhile. I can't pretend that children are not interested in gender or affected by gender differences, but I don't have to let the answers they get from the culture about gender be the final word. Early childhood educators have a unique opportunity to help children discover a more positive way to view themselves and the opposite sex.

For more on gender role development, see the following:

Beal, Carole R. *Boys and Girls: The Development of Gender Roles.* Columbus, OH, McGraw Hill, 1993.

Kindlon, Daniel J., and Michael Thompson. *Raising Cain: Protecting the Emotional Life of Boys.* New York: Ballantine Books, 1999.

Miedzian, Myriam. *Boys Will Be Boys: Breaking the Link between Masculinity and Violence.* New York: Lantern Books, 2002.

Paley, Vivian Gussin. *Boys and Girls: Superheroes in the Doll Corner.* Chicago: University of Chicago Press, 1984.

STORIES FROM THE CLASSROOM

Leopards, Lions, and Tigers

As children grow, their play changes, sometimes in ways that parents and staff would rather avoid. That can set up staff and parent conflicts. Depending on how the changes are handled, they can either undermine school cohesion or solidify it. Here's the story of how one child's play started a dialogue that resulted in months of dramatic play and a stronger bond among parents and staff.

All winter long, my classroom had been filled with cats and kittens. Painted whiskers, yarn tails, neck and wrist bells, and hair bands with old shoulder pads attached for ears were all the fashion. Boys and girls alike licked their paws, played with balls of yarn, stretched, purred, and rubbed up against legs. Mama and Papa cats curled up on pillows and snuggled their babies. Children found new ways to climb the playground equipment. We had several cat circles where we sang our favorite songs by meowing them, and we had a cat snack with cheese cubes and bowls of water to lick. Pets visited regularly, and a vet brought a box of kittens and talked about their care. Occasionally, we had a hissing confrontation with claws out, or a howling match (one parent suggested throwing old shoes at them). For the most part, though, my cats were peaceful and sweet and everyone was satisfied.

Spring came, and I knew that my adorable kittens were growing into something less tame when five-year-old Dora spoke to me:

Dora: Growl! I'm part kitten and part leopard.

Me: Which part is leopard?

Dora: The part that bites heads off.

Dora had discovered a leopard shirt in our dress-up clothes, and as soon as she put it on she became a mean, snarling, hungry wildcat. She soon had a whole pride of leopards, lions, and tigers at her command.

Dora had always been a charismatic and assertive leader, but as a mama cat she was willing to compromise, include, and forgive. As a leopard queen, Dora became a play dictator. No one else could make decisions.

Anyone who didn't meet her standards was excluded from play. Any child who defied her was verbally harassed. She and her gang disrupted circles and meals with cat screams.

And heaven help you if Dora decided you were prey. She would tell her wildcat gang to attack and devour children without warning, whether they were interested in being part of the game or not. (Dora, it turned out, had been watching the Discovery Channel with her older sister.) The rest of the class developed a nervous watchfulness, like a herd of antelope at a watering hole.

Younger children were complaining at home and refusing to come to school. Children who were part of the wildcat gang were growling at their parents at home. Alarmed parents wanted to know what was going on. Why were we letting this play continue? Why was Dora even allowed to stay in the class? Who was in charge, Dora or the teachers?

The staff spent an evening discussing how to respond to the play and to parents' concerns. "We have to stop them," one teacher said. "They're being unsafe, and parents are too upset." Several others agreed.

"Hold on," I said. "What is actually happening that is unsafe? Can we change that behavior without banning the play? What are the children getting out of this?"

When we shared what we had observed about the play, one fact stood out: while children were being intimidated, the wildcats rarely hurt anyone physically. Even when they were stalking and pouncing on children, there was lots of noise and pretend scratching and biting, but very little actual contact. Dora led this performance, and her followers copied it. This was a step forward for several of the children involved, who would have been unable to stop themselves from getting too physical only a few months before. As often happens, when children stop using their bodies to express anger and other feelings and start using their words (just like we ask them to), the result is not always pleasant. While it was clear we had to place limits on the verbal harassment and threatening gestures, we also had to acknowledge the growth we saw.

We also noticed that there were two kinds of attacks. One was when the wildcats forced their game on people without permission, although it was not always easy to tell if some of the victims were upset or if they were screaming for the fun of it. The other was when they excluded other children, either by growling at them or by stepping out of their wildcat roles to tell them to go away. The cats seemed to use both kinds of attacks to feel more powerful as a group, but the first kind was also being used to extend the play without trying to hurt anyone.

What were the positive impulses we could support in this play? We made a list:

• As wildcats, the children were challenging themselves physically and using their bodies more creatively than when they were kittens— climbing, balancing, jumping, running, and doing gymnastics.

• The group was feeling powerful by bonding together in an exciting shared game.

• Children were energized by their new ability to imagine themselves in fantasy roles.

• Some of the children were showing an interest in facts about wildcats and their habitats.

• Dora was helping children stay physically safe.

We also made a list of behaviors that we wanted to change:

• Wildcats needed clear permission from other children before hunting them.

• The cats needed a way to define themselves as a powerful group without intimidating others.

• The staff had to make it clear that adults were in charge and would keep everyone safe.

• Children couldn't come to circle or meal times as wildcats until they could do it safely.

Then the staff brainstormed curriculum ideas that would support children's positive impulses while allowing the staff to institute new rules. They came up with the following:

• Adding books, photos, and other information about real wildcats to several areas of the room and to an outdoor quiet space

- Using a water table half full of dirt to create a jungle scene, with small plastic wildcats, rocks, sticks, and clippings of evergreen trees and other plants

- Creating a defined area on the playground for the play and setting up climbing challenges in it

- Planning art projects that would allow the children to make costumes and props

The next day, we posted these lists outside the classroom with a note to parents about how they were created. I tried to check in with all the parents who had expressed concern about the play. Most were relieved to see that we were taking positive steps to contain the problems, although some were leery of our ideas and still wanted the play banned. I asked them to let us know what their children were saying at home, to give us some time to institute changes, and to help us judge whether our changes were working.

Over the next few days we set aside one quarter of the yard as a wildcat preserve, using colored rope to mark the area. We added large boxes for dens, along with tires and log chunks for balancing. We created an obstacle course where it was safe to run on four legs. We brought in books about wildcats, and the vet came back to talk about the difference between pet care and wild animal care. The jungle water table was a big hit, not with the children who had been wildcats but with several of the children who had been afraid of it.

We also set up rules and discussed them at several circles, using puppets to play them out:

- Wildcats can growl and fight and hunt only in the Wildcat Corner.

- If you are inside the Wildcat Corner, you are playing the game. If you don't want to play, don't enter.

- Everyone is allowed in the Wildcat Corner.

- No real biting or scratching, even in the Wildcat Corner.

- No wildcats are allowed at circle time, meals, or naptime.

- Wildcats can only hunt children who want to be hunted.

The last rule brought up several issues. Several parents, and a few staff, were appalled by the sight of children pretending to take down and eat another child, even if everyone consented. Some thought it was unsafe, because now that the wildcats had their own jungle, they were gang-tackling their meals. The last problem was that it was not clear who wanted to be hunter and who wanted to be prey.

We decided to engage the children in solving these problems. After looking at books, children decided that the preferred meal for lions, tigers, and leopards was gazelle, although the younger children just called them deer. But how do you know who wants to be a gazelle? How do you hunt them and tackle them without hurting anyone? We solved the first problem by making costumes. The leopards, lions, and tigers wanted spots and stripes and manes. We couldn't buy wildcat furs or more face paints because we had used up our supply budget, but Dora realized she could cut out black paper spots and tape them to her clothes and body. We stopped children from drawing all over themselves with markers. Others discovered that they could use colored tape to create tiger stripes. New styles of tails and ears followed. The art area was buzzing.

Lion manes were a bigger challenge. Children tried yarn and strips of paper and cloth taped to headbands, but the fringe kept getting in their faces and the costumes were soon abandoned. We were more successful with necklaces make out of wide lengths of fabric, with strips cut along one edge. With the addition of some shaggy brown wigs, the lions were satisfied.

Gazelles were happy with lightweight ponchos made of brown cloth. They wanted long horns, too, but the staff vetoed that idea. Even short horns seemed to encourage head butting. Someone read about zebras, and a family donated a few fake furs in black and white stripes, so we ended up with a mixed herd. We added a new rule: Only children wearing costumes inside the Wildcat Corner could be hunted. We solved the safety problem by adding a couple of mats at the edge of the Wildcat Corner. Gazelle could be chased and caught anywhere, but they could only be tackled and devoured on the mats.

We were surprised at how many children chose the experience of being hunted. Even Dora tried it and pronounced it fun, which led all of her wildcats to take turns as victims. They also demanded more information about the prey. After reading about them, we created high jumping places for gazelles, and they started crouching down together in herds.

Dora became fascinated by a picture of a leopard sleeping in a tree. She wanted to sleep that way at naptime, so she arranged blankets and pillows over a row of large blocks and slept with her arms hanging over the sides. We loosened the rule about wildcats at nap when she showed she was able to play the role without bothering anyone else. We soon had children sleeping on a variety of chairs, benches, and other "tree branches," their heads full of dreams of basking in the sun after a heavy meal of zebra.

While many on the staff were skeptical of this curriculum at first, they were won over by the ability of the children to play the game safely. The time we had spent with the children making sure their cat and kitten games were safe paid off. Dora's leadership blossomed as she learned that she could play a game that was wild and exciting without being mean or dangerous.

Some of the parents were not so sure. We devoted a good portion of a parent meeting to the discussion, going over our goals and the rules we had set up, and listening to parents' concerns and ideas. We agreed to make sure no one felt pressured to participate, to encourage children to try out both roles, to be very clear about where the fantasy play stopped and real life began, and to have several other curriculum strands available for the children who had no interest in the play. They let us know that they had been uncomfortable with their children licking from bowls during our cat snack, and that they didn't want us to try a wildcat snack at all. Most of the parents accepted our explanations; some continued to be critical, and told their children not to participate. We agreed to tell those children that their parents wanted them to play other games.

We were particularly concerned about Adrian's parents. Adrian was one of the most enthusiastic tigers, and his parents were dedicated pacifists and vegetarians. They surprised us, though, by being supportive of the play. The only thing they asked was that we talk with the children about the differences between animals' and people's reasons for hunting. We invited the mother to come to a circle time with the agreement that she wouldn't tell children that hunting was bad (several of the families went hunting regularly) and she accepted. She explained that people can choose what they eat, and that she chose to eat only plants, because she didn't like to hurt animals. Two children went home and told their parents that they wanted to be vegetarians.

The wildcat game continued for about six weeks. Children got tired of being the prey after a month, so the cats started hunting stuffed animals, and then imaginary ones. They still wanted to try out the new climbing challenges we added to the Wildcat Corner every week. Occasionally other wild animals like bears and wolves would appear, but the staff didn't want to put effort into supporting them, and they disappeared.

We could tell it was time to dismantle the Wildcat Corner when Dora announced, "I'm not a leopard, I'm Catwoman." That was our first clue about what we would be doing most of the summer.

By observing children carefully to separate out what we should encourage and what we should stop, talking to parents and taking their concerns seriously, creating interesting play areas and other curriculum, and setting up some new rules, we were able to take play that was potentially divisive and dangerous and turn it into a fun learning experience that helped make everyone feel a part of our classroom community.

Conclusion

Whenever I do a workshop or class about superhero play, someone wants me to tell them the right way to respond to it. The right way would be to create a world where violence and racism are universally condemned and people who use them are kept from power, a world where peacemaking becomes the model for children's play. If children were never exposed to brutality, bias, and other abuses of power, our jobs as teachers would be much simpler, but that solution isn't within easy reach. All our work aimed at fighting these problems will be imperfect as long as there are people and institutions that depend on violence to maintain their status and wealth. It's easy to get caught up in arguments with parents and staff and forget that the conflict continues because of these absent participants, who refuse to join in making this a better world for children. Still, when parents and teachers cooperate, we can at least make that peaceful vision come true on a smaller scale in our classrooms, so children can get a glimpse of what a peaceful and fair world might look like.

Teaching is about creating that respectful community and allowing children to grow into who they want to be. More and more, teaching is seen as a one-way street, with teachers filling students with important information. I can't teach that way. I know there are skills children need to function in our world, and I want the children in my classrooms to gain that knowledge. But I also know that children are busy creating their own vision of what should happen next in their lives, and they will share that with us through their play if we take the time to watch and listen.

As you can tell from this book, I enjoy children's dramatic play, and I take particular pleasure in helping children create stories for their play. You may not share my enthusiasm for these activities. That's okay. What's important is that you have something you love—art, music, science, poetry, or whatever—and share that passion with children. I don't mean you can ignore other subjects. I believe that an effective teacher can use their passion as an anchor to teach about literacy, math, positive social relationships, problem-solving skills, emotions, and everything else children need to learn. It's your own, unique love of learning that will impress preschoolers, more than any facts you can teach them.

However you choose to teach, your job is to listen to children's dreams for the future and support them in ways that help both the children and the world mature. Superhero play is one of the ways your children say, "This is how I want to live. Can you help me?" You can help them transform themselves into the powerful and respectful people they want to become. In the process, they will help you transform into the powerful and respectful teacher you want to become. Teaching works best when it is an exchange of gifts.

Some additional resources on superhero play:

Carlsson-Paige, Nancy, and Diane E. Levin. *The War Play Dilemma: Balancing Needs and Values in the Early Childhood Classroom.* New York: Teachers College Press, 1987.

Carlsson-Paige, Nancy, and Diane E. Levin. *Who's Calling the Shots: How to Respond Effectively to Children's Fascination with War Play and War Toys.* Gabriola Island, BC, Canada: New Society Publishers, 1990.

Jones, Gerard. *Killing Monsters: Why Children Need Fantasy, Superheroes, and Make-Believe Violence.* New York: Basic Books, 2002.

Paley, Vivian Gussin. *Bad Guys Don't Have Birthdays: Fantasy Play at Four.* Chicago: University of Chicago Press, 1988.

Index

Other Resources from Redleaf Press

Changing Channels: Activities Promoting Media Smarts and Creative Problem Solving for Kids
by Eric Hoffman. Find positive ways to help children understand what they see on TV and in other forms of media. With the Parents' Choice Award-winning CD by Cathy Fink and Marcy Marxer, these activities help children think critically, resolve conflicts productively, and develop healthy self-esteem.

Best Day of the Week
by Nancy Carlsson-Paige. The story of Angela and Calvin and how they resolve their play-related differences constructively.

The Optimistic Classroom: Creative Ways to Give Children Hope
by Deborah Hewitt and Sandra Heidemann. Over seventy activities will develop ten strengths that allow children to meet and cope with the challenges they face.

That's Not Fair! A Teacher's Guide to Activism with Young Children
by Ann Pelo and Fran Davidson. Real-life stories of activist children, combined with teachers' experiences and reflections, create a complete guide to supporting children's response to unfairness.

Heroines and Heroes/ Heroínas y héroes
by Eric Hoffman, with illustrations by Judi Rosen. A story about how leadership, bravery, and strength are not limited by gender. Adventurous Kayla rescues Nate during their imaginative superhero play. Heroines and heroes to the rescue!

Best Best Colors/Los mejores colores
by Eric Hoffman, with illustrations by Celeste Henriquez. When asked about his favorite color, Nate doesn't know what to say. When his friends say he has to choose one best friend, it just doesn't seem possible. With the help of his two mammas, Nate learns he can have more than one best color and one best friend.

Play Lady/La señora juguetona
by Eric Hoffman, with illustrations by Suzanne Tornquist. Her name is Jane Kurosawa, but the children call her Play Lady. When someone vandalizes Play Lady's home and property, the children in her neighborhood lend a helping hand. This is a moving story about how children can cope with a hate crime in their own neighborhood.

No Fair to Tigers/No es justo para los tigres
by Eric Hoffman, with illustrations by Janice Lee Porter. When Mandy goes to the store to buy tiger treats, the three steps out front make it impossible for her to get her wheelchair inside. This story about a girl with a disability and her stuffed tiger shows how they ask for fair treatment and offers solutions to the problems they encounter.